A HISTORY OF
FANS AND
FANDOM

To everyone who has ever been a told 'that's a bit much isn't it?'
about the thing they love.
And to Bousha, for the 'Holly Shelf'.

A HISTORY OF FANS AND FANDOM

A Journey into the Passion and Power of Fan Culture

HOLLY SWINYARD

WHITE OWL

AN IMPRINT OF PEN & SWORD BOOKS LTD.
YORKSHIRE – PHILADELPHIA

First published in Great Britain in 2024 by
PEN AND SWORD WHITE OWL
An imprint of
Pen & Sword Books Ltd
Yorkshire - Philadelphia

ISBN 978 1 39904 283 3

Typeset in 11/15 pts Sabon by
SJmagic DESIGN SERVICES, India.

Printed and bound in India by Parksons Graphics Pvt. Ltd.

Pen & Sword Books Ltd. incorporates the imprints of Pen & Sword Books: After the Battle, Archaeology, Atlas, Aviation, Battleground, Discovery, Family History, History, Maritime, Military, Politics, Select, Transport, True Crime, Fiction, Frontline Books, Leo Cooper, Praetorian Press, Seaforth Publishing, Wharncliffe and White Owl.

For a complete list of Pen & Sword titles please contact

PEN & SWORD BOOKS LIMITED
George House, Beevor Street, Off Pontefract Road, Hoyle Mill, Barnsley, South Yorkshire, England, S71 1HN.
E-mail: enquiries@pen-and-sword.co.uk
Website: www.pen-and-sword.co.uk

or

PEN AND SWORD BOOKS
1950 Lawrence Rd, Havertown, PA 19083, USA
E-mail: uspen-and-sword@casematepublishers.com
Website: www.penandswordbooks.com

CONTENTS

Introduction		7
QUESTION ONE WHEN?		20
Chapter 1	Fandom will, err... Find a Way	23
Chapter 2	The Future is Now: Moving into the Twentieth Century	41
Chapter 3	To Go Where No Fan Has Gone Before	52
Chapter 4	Let's Get Connected	63
QUESTION TWO WHY?		69
Chapter 1	Modern Myth	72
Chapter 2	A Touch of Familiarity	82
Chapter 3	Welcome to the Tribe	86
QUESTIONS THREE AND FOUR WHO? AND HOW?		98
Chapter 1	Affirmative and Transformative	100
Chapter 2	Performance as a Fanwork	118
Chapter 3	Roll For Initiative: Tabletop Roleplaying Games	138
QUESTION FIVE WHERE?		149
Chapter 1	Have You Tried Turning it Off and Online Again?	151
Chapter 2	Space Invaders	167
Chapter 3	As Above, So Below	181
Chapter 4	Creator and Fan: Finding the Balance	188

QUESTION SIX   HUH?   195

Chapter 1   Culture Wars: GamerGate   197

Chapter 2   Change My Dear and Not a Moment Too Soon   205

Chapter 3   Look Inside the House   214

Chapter 4   Learn From History or be Doomed to Repeat It   218

QUESTION SEVEN   THE END?   223

Further Reading   225

Glossary   228

INTRODUCTION

What is Fandom?

I would like to assume that you have picked up this book in some hopes of that question being answered. So, I'll give you the answer.

Fandom, as according to the *Cambridge Dictionary*, means:

> The state of being a fan of someone or something, especially a very enthusiastic one: 'the world of martial arts movie fandom'.

Right. There you go. That was easy.

You can put this book down and go read something else in the shop now; there's probably something by Neil Gaiman nearby you can flick through. He's very good, making all those TV shows; people run conventions about his stuff, you know. Dress up and everything, whole blogs and fanzines and not very well-hidden references in book titles dedicated to... ah, I think we might have been a bit hasty.

Come back here and maybe hold fire on putting the book down just yet. I feel that, as wonderful as the *Cambridge Dictionary* might be, along with all the other single line definitions that are taking up some small amount of ink or data, this is somewhat missing the point.

Let's start again.

One Small Note

I want to jump in here, before we start the book proper – it is coming I promise – to give you a quick message. There is going to be a lot of terminology throughout the book that refers to fan culture and not everyone is going to know all of that. In fact, there may well have been something already and there will definitely be some in the introduction that's on the next page. Do not be alarmed, or worried, you are reading this book to learn about fandom after all, it would be foolish of me to assume that you, dear reader, know all these words, but nor do I want to assume you don't know them by over explaining.

So! What you will find, after the introduction that is about to happen, honestly, is a list of some of the terminology that will be used at length throughout the chapters to follow, and also at the end of the book a glossary of as many terms as I can think to put in.

Or you can just *Clockwork Orange* this thing and see how long it takes you work out what the words mean from context. And wouldn't I love to know the outcome of that fun experiment?

Okay! Introduction, on we go!

No Really, What is Fandom?

I have, as have many people, including quite a few of you reading this book I would wager, been part of fandom in various ways throughout my life. I've gone from a brief and passing fancy in a new piece of media to cross my path, to having my feet dangling over the edge of a fandom precipice, daring myself to take the plunge and learn more, all the way up to swimming in some deep and, shall we say, interesting waters. There are fandoms that have held my gaze my whole life, and ones that burnt bright in my esteem but faded as quickly as they came. And, as I said, I am far from the only one.

Each of us will have those things that we love, whether we recognise it as fandom or not: the football club where you never miss a game, the pilgrimage you take to see your favourite band every year, the money you invest in your golf clubs/limited edition vinyl/hi-tech gaming set up/Disneyland annual pass/personal passion of your choice (please delete as appropriate) that you share with other like-minded people in one way or another. This is fandom. You are, on some level, partaking in fan culture, and you didn't even know it.

It might not be the image that pops into your head when you think about fans. You know what I mean, that image of screaming girls, hysterical to see the handsome pop star(s) that are currently holding the heart throb position in the media, or spotty boys in basements full of perfectly packaged action figure collections, but it all comes down to the same thing in the end: there are some things in your world that you love and want to share that love in some way. And no, not your dog. Though I'm pretty sure someone could make an argument for Crufts lining up with the qualities of fandom in one way or another. I'm right though, aren't I? That's what you thought of. I'm looking forward to dissuading you of these ideas, one of which is more than a little bit problematic, and well rooted in sexism and the mocking of the opinions of teenage girls. See me in Question Two, we will be having words. Lots of them – plus, there's nothing wrong with collecting.

There is this idea that fan culture is a part of youth culture and that simply isn't true. Turning thirty doesn't automatically wipe our brains of any excitement we had about the new season of *Game of Thrones* coming out, to be replaced with a desire to knit quietly in a corner – I recommend knitting with intent while you watch some Targaryen set fire to a person with a dragon and doing something questionable with a relative – or mean we walk away from the 40,000-word fanfic we were writing in favour of doing taxes. But even if it is the case that you aren't all that interested in getting into the depths of fandom discourse and are happy sitting in the shallow end of the pool does not mean you aren't part of the bigger summer splash day that is fan culture – see Question Two for Dr Vivian Asimos' 'Pool Theory'.

It's all fandom, all the way down.

We can't seem to escape the urge to put our passions on a pedestal. No matter how hard we try to call it 'childish', 'silly' or 'cringe', the instinct to celebrate remains deep rooted in us all. But what is it that makes humans so invested in things that we create these groups, our little tribes, this fan culture?

It's not something new either, though you'd be forgiven for thinking that it was brought about through the age of the internet and the explosion of growth that fandom has seen since the first message boards and newsletters went online. We tend to forget that people in the past were people too, they weren't all living in black and white without interests or passions or funny little hobbies that others considered eccentric; humans have very much always been human-ing.

Manias around famous people or works are not a new fad, you can look to Byron or Shakespeare and easily see that. Nor is collecting items of memorabilia in order to show your love and share ideas about these things with your fellow devotees a twentieth century invention, and there's definitely an argument for fanart and fiction existing long before you could commission it on Twitter – at time of writing Twitter was in the midst of the Elon Musk take-over. Author note: While proofing this book Twitter became X. I will still be referring to it was Twitter despite it being the website formerly known as I will be interested to see if this comment remains relevant in the next few years – or in a tag on Ao3 (Archive Of Our Own). In the words of Mark Twain:

> 'There is no such thing as a new idea. It is impossible. We simply take a lot
> of old ideas and put them into a sort of mental kaleidoscope.'

Fandom as it currently stands is the next branch on the tree, growing out of the ideas of those who came before us. I would be prepared to put good money on a Victorian being able to understand Tumblr as similar to a commonplace book, or an Elizabethan seeing the ups and downs of a true crime podcast as the same as the plays on that very same subject that happened on stages just down the road from where the crimes happened! The more you look the easier it is to see that we've always had this funny impulse to collectively share in things beyond the simple everyday tasks of living. It's almost like our brains really want something to grab hold of purely for enjoyment's sake, and fandom fills that gap rather nicely.

Still not much closer to understanding what it is though.

That is why this book exists. Because I wanted to find out what fandom really was, under the surface, and let me tell you, the tip of this iceberg is nothing compared to the beast of a kaiju that I found hidden beneath it. There are fandoms to things you have never heard of that take up vast spans of YouTube and Twitter; there are fandoms that seem to sleep like dragons waiting for a piece of new media to come along, calling them to rise from their slumber; there are fandoms within fandoms like endless Russian dolls getting forever more niche; there are fandoms that have been at war with themselves since their conception and yet are still completely beloved by those within them; and there is so, *so*, SO much more.

There's the meta – no not the Facebook thing, rather to be self-referential, don't worry, remember there's that terminology list in the next few pages! – about fandom. Analytical work collecting and discussing how fandom works, reams and reams of it across so many media, where the ins and outs of all fan culture are discussed whilst also delving into the tiniest minutiae of an individual piece of media, or even fan work, to pull it apart like a somewhat worrying kid prodding the innards of a dead dove on the street. Gosh, this very book is part of the meta of fandom, and isn't it just chock full of as many references as possible to make sure that you know that.

With all of this, and this brief description does not do what it describes justice at all, I still don't think that answers the question. And clearly, this isn't being asked for the first time, and definitely not by me. There are a myriad of intelligent people out there devoting their lives to the study of fandom, people who link into fandom in so many different ways, all of them dedicated to not just their own fan communities but also to the larger thought of what it is that they are doing as part of them. Some of them were patient enough to talk to me for my misadventure into this TARDIS of a subject, and almost all of them told me 'Oof, that's a big subject you've got there.' And by golly, they are right in that assertion. The thing is, I can't stop asking the question, none of us can – it's possible I should have listened to the folks who made this subject their whole careers, but where would be the fun in that?

I have posed that to myself on multiple occasions throughout the years, out of genuine curiosity for the most part. Before I considered writing a book on the subject, I have found myself trying to work out what this thing I had dedicated much of my teenage, and I'll be honest, adult years to. But it never quite settled into one from inside my head. Also, to my poor friends who have had to listen to me ruminate on this subject for years. I'm sorry, I owe you all a drink.

I found myself in a similar position when I began work on a set of books about the cosplay community – if you don't know much about cosplay don't worry, I'll be touching on that in this book too – it came up over and over: why were people dressing up, what was it for? Doesn't much answer the question that, does it?

This is advanced warning by the way, and an apology. It's really hard for me to not talk about cosplay. It's one of the most interesting sub-cultures of the twentieth and twenty-first centuries and I will go on at length if you don't stop me. So, I'm stopping myself now until later, where I may allow myself a paragraph or two if I'm good – well because it's a sub-culture fandom.

Seeing fandoms grow from nothing – in some cases quite literally – then blossom with art, fics, discussive works and a simple shared love which then, so often, begins to edge into discourse or in-fighting before settling into the steady rhythm of an ecosystem with each area playing its part to keep the beast that is a fandom going; it is confounding and fascinating in equal measure. It's organic, cyclical almost. Fandoms come and go, regrow with reboots on roots set by someone maybe decades before. Some of these fandoms remain in the wider cultural zeitgeist: *Star Wars*, *The Lord of the Rings*, *Star Trek*, and *Doctor Who* would be the most obvious, but you'd be surprised by how many things you've never heard of are affecting the way that pop culture moves forward without the mainstream even realising the rock just under the surface of the water that's changing its path – *Undertale* whomst? And all the while there are others that fade entirely, huge Hollywood blockbusters that never leave more than a speck on the cultural landscape, and with the rest taking up a space somewhere in between, roaming the planes as a cult classic or a fan favourite.

It's almost impossible to guess what will become a fandom, though plenty of people have tried; marketing folks especially would love to know the secret to a successful fandom, but as with all things you can't predict what will succeed. In any environment no matter how well nurtured a plant or encouraged an animal, there is never any guarantee it will flourish. All the while a weed growing out from the patio may well succeed in spite of your best efforts to get rid of it. I've pushed this metaphor a little far but life, er…, will find a way, and so will fandom. Where you least expect it too.

So what is it that brings all of this together into something that we understand as fandom?

The more I thought about it, the more I came to realise that it was a question with no easy ending. This is often the case with hobbies or countercultures like this. Because the thing is, you can say 'fandom is this' and use that dictionary definition, or whatever definition you pick out of all the myriad of phrasings that are out there to say the same thing; you could write an essay on the subject full of sources and studies, and hey, you could even write a whole book – and I am most certainly not the first or the last to do just that – and you'd still have a way to go before you understood it.

It took thinking all these thoughts, going around on the little merry-go-round in my head, trying with all my might to get off the ride, when it hit me. Or more exactly snuck up on me over the course of a few goes around: it's not one question, it's six.

Who, What, Where, When, Why and How. Though possibly not in that order for the circumstances of this book.

In fact, let's take it in this order:

What? What is Fandom? – That's this bit you're reading right now, hello!
When? When did Fandom begin?

Why? Why do people get into Fandom?

Who and How? Who does Fandom and How do they do it?

Where? Where do people enjoy Fandom?

Each of these questions will be tackled as we go along, chapter by chapter, to see if we can answer them. Nice, little (ish) bites to try and get to the bottom of this whole fandom thing. Though, these questions still don't catch the nuance so if we slide a bit off topic as we search for the answers, please forgive me, I just found something interesting to go and wander off after. Like finding a rare butterfly when you're meant to be trekking for buried treasure or a petrified orange (if you get this reference, you're going to enjoy Question Four).

But as they always say it's the journey not the destination, so I hope that this will be an enjoyable jaunt of discovery whatever it is we find at the end. Maybe if we're lucky we will come to some sort of answer together, or perhaps we will all find separate ideas that satisfy us. Or we will be none the wiser but with a lot more knowledge shoved in our heads to talk about at the next Christmas party or family dinner, and I am never one to discourage an info dump, but apologies to those on the receiving end in advance.

Okay, all ready? Onwards we go.

Some Useful Terminology

Before we trek off into the 'here be monsters' area of the world, it might be worth picking up a map with a few guiding points to make sure we don't get too lost. Best to know the language of the world you're stepping into, or at least have a phrase book.

Remember what I said just before the introduction about there being useful words? This is that bit so feel free to skip on ahead if you're doing the *Clockwork Orange* read through. See you at Question One.

While there is a glossary in the back of the book to help you with some of the terms that will be thrown around throughout our little journey, I felt it worthwhile going a bit more in depth with some of the words that (a) will be used more than others and (b) have some level of importance within the discussion of fandom and fandom studies in general. Some of them will pop up a lot – two in particular. In fact they get a whole chapter of discussion, and I promise you it, it's nowhere near as boring as you might think. But I would say that, I'm writing the book – so rather than just throwing you in the deep end and hoping you know how to swim, or at least float, in the jargon, I'm going to give you a nice stripy rubber ring of understanding to keep you going.

Some of these you may think 'hang on, I know that! I am reading this book after all!' but for the sake of clarity and everyone being on the same page, literally – you bet I'm laughing at my own rubbish jokes throughout all of this – let's do the thing.

Affirmative Fandom

The opposite to Transformative Fandom. Sort of. I will be going into more depth on this subject later on so don't worry if you are scratching you head over this term but let me give you a quick idea of what it is.

Affirmative Fandom is one of the two types of fandom that is defined within fan studies and fan spaces. Affirmative Fandom tends to refer to fans who are creator-centric, and who collect, analyse, archive, and affirm the canon of media. Examples of affirmative fandom could be The Tolkien Society, community events such as WorldCon or critical works on a topic of media.

Blorbo

Short for 'Blorbo from my shows'.

A term coined on 24 December 2021 by Tumblr user thelustiestargonianmaid (yes really) that was initially meant to mock fandom behaviour of talking about their favourite characters, often having strange names, completely out of context and at the drop of a hat, if not less. However, in true fandom style, it has since been taken and used by fans as a useful, short-hand descriptor for their personal favourites whilst recognising that others may not understand, as well as indulging a little in the enjoyable levels of silliness that exist in fan culture.

Other terms for similar characters include 'Glup Shitto' and 'Scrimblo Bimblo'. And anyone who is a fan of any fantasy or sci-fi franchise knows that these names are about as reasonable as any. I mean, I got excited to see Gungi, the Wookie padawan from *Star Wars: The Clone Wars* show up in *The Bad Batch* trailer, because he is my Blorbo, from my shows.

This term is not even a year old at time of writing, but I am including it here rather than in the glossary at the back, as, honestly, I think it's going to stick around in fandom terminology.

Canon

This is the material within a piece of fiction that is officially accepted as part of the story by the fans that fanworks are then based around.

Creator

The person or people who create or work on the media that people are fans of.

   This is not a universal definition at all, but it is a definition I am going to use in this book in order to differentiate between fans and those making the media. E.g., they were big fans of the creator of *Sonic the Hedgehog*.

Cosplay

Had to put it in here somewhere now, didn't I?

   A subcultural form of fanwork that takes the form of dressing up as characters you are a fan of. Many make their own costumes, while others buy or modify, in order to show their love for the character and the media said character comes from. It can involve performing, photography, videography, community groups and social media, with people sharing their passion and their process with each other.

Fanart

Art created by fans for the consumption of other fans in their fandoms and community spaces. It is done for the personal enjoyment of the artist, with the hope that of those within their fandom, often a specific circle of that fandom, will also enjoy it, e.g. people who ship – bear with me, ship and shipping is defined on the next page – of Captain America and Tony Stark will want to see art or make art of that ship and share it with others who like it too. Sometimes artists will monetise their work by selling prints, stickers, and other small-scale merch.

Fandom

Head back to that first page. Then come back here and continue reading.

Fanfiction

Fiction of all kinds created by fans for the consumption of other fans in their fandoms and community spaces. It can range from short hundred-word flash fiction to novel length epics, poetry and song lyrics, and cover just as many genres, themes and subjects. Much like fanart, it is done for the personal enjoyment of the creator, their fandom, and those with the same specific likes within the fan space. While sometimes it is monetised, this is far less common than with fanart.

Fanzine

A small publication made by fans for fans, of a particular performer, group, or form of entertainment. Often called 'zines for short, the creators of these publications are usually amateurs and come together to share their fanart, fanfiction and meta essays on the subject of the 'zine. 'Zines range in production value from self-photocopied and stapled pamphlets to book-style publications. They can also be digital and shared online or passed around on offline memory devices. They are normally not for profit, either being sent out for free or with sales going to a chosen charity once the cost of production is covered.

Fangirl and Fanboy

Fans.

Okay. Let's talk about this.

These are terms that started as gendered descriptors, but over the years they have become much more interchangeable to mean the same thing and the original gendered nature of them is more ignored in favour of behaviour description. There are some arguments that 'fangirl' and 'fangirling' refers to a type of fan that is more likely to be loud, over the top, and excitable in their attentions, with 'fanboy' and 'fanboying' being a more canon-obsessed, analytical and collection-orientated. These do fall into the binary views of gender and behaviour, so it is worth pointing out that the definition of both words when you google them are pretty much the same.

- **Fangirl** (from the Oxford Languages definition):

noun
a female fan, especially one who is obsessive about comics, film, music, or science fiction.
'your average fangirl, despite the implication of the name, is a grown-up'
verb
(of a female fan) behave in an obsessive or overexcited way.
'I'm still fangirling over this casting'

- **Fanboy** (from the Oxford Languages definition):

noun

a male fan, especially one who is obsessive about comics, music, movies, or science fiction.

verb

(of a male fan) behave in an obsessive or overexcited way.
'he fanboyed out meeting his idol on the red carpet'

See?

For the most part you are likely to see these terms being used in fan spaces interchangeably or used as a gendered term of choice by the individual using them. I will tend to use 'fan' throughout the book but not exclusively.

Meta

To be self-referential. Meta works are fan-authored analytical, non-fiction pieces of fanwork or discussions that take an in-depth look at a piece of media, be that the original source of the fandom, or of a fanwork – do you think the word fan will lose its meaning before we reach the end of the book?

Ship/Shipper/Shipping

Short for 'relationship' or 'relationshipper' and coined in 1996 by the *X-Files* fandom, a ship is two or more characters who are paired together in a romantic or sexual way by fans, often with its own unique name, e.g. Destiel for Dean Winchester and Castiel from *Supernatural*. These ships can be both canonical within the piece of media or non-canonical. Shipping is the act of bring those characters together, often through fanart and fanfic, with a shipper being the person who wants to see those characters together.

Squee

Little bit of an old school term, but it's a noise of excitement. It's high pitched, and often in regard to your favourite character, ship or fanwork, though it can also be used in reaction to real people and a piece of media itself.

Commonly associated with fangirls over fanboys but it has become a general online term that now tends to be used in a more tongue-in-cheek way but not exclusively.

Example: Sasuke (from *Naruto*) totally makes me squee! Oh, the flashbacks to my teens are strong.

Transformative Fandom

The opposite to Affirmative Fandom. Kind of.

Transformative Fandom is one of the two types of fandom that is defined within fan studies and fan spaces. Transformative, or Transformational Fandom covers fanfic, fanart, cosplay, roleplay – any fan-centric activities or works that adapt or challenge the canon in some way or create new things around it. This can even include making creations with crochet, filming fan-films for YouTube, or making music about your favourite video games. It's fans finding new and creative ways to play around with canon however they see fit.

One, small addition to this...

Acronyms

No, it doesn't have another meaning in fandom, its more that fans love acronyms. Can't get enough of them. Shows, franchises, ships, characters, memes, online jargon, each other, all of this will have acronyms, and being that this a book about all fandom fun, it will be including a fair few.

This is your only warning. Joking. But do keep your eyes peeled for acronyms popping up.

Example: This is a discussion of the Marvel Cinematic Universe (MCU), so it will be the acronym that will be used for the rest of the discussion.

Before we move on...

When writing this book, I made the conscious decision that I would not talk in depth about sports or music fandom. This was purely for the reason that I had to draw the line somewhere since the magnitude of the project I was taking on suddenly became very obvious to me and, while there is nothing wrong with these two areas and I will touch on them where needed or where it is important to do so, I felt it best to give myself something more of a focus. Plus, I will hold my hands up to this right now, I'm a big old nerd, give me space lasers and a magic piece of jewellery over a sports ball any day of the week.

Sorry all! Though I won't say no to a good day at the Tour de France, but that is besides the point.

That being said, I would like to direct you towards a few books on the subjects of sports and music fandoms in order to round off your education of fandom and fan culture properly, and I have always wanted to give out a reading list. On top of what is listed below, in the back of this book you will find a reading list for each chapter, and I very much encourage you, if you are interested in learning more to give those books a go.

Sports

Unsurprisingly many of the sports books have a focus on football (both versions) since team sports tend to gather the most intense support base. You will find many a common thread between the sports team fanatic and the Marvel Cinematic Universe (MCU) lover, but these aren't the only sports to have their fans.

- *The Ethics of Sports Fandom* by Adam Kadlac
- *A Fan's Life: The Agony of Victory and the Thrill of Defeat* by Paul Campos
- *The I in Team: Sports Fandom and the Reproduction of Identity* by Erin C. Tarver

Music

Music fandom tends to split into groups for individual artists, Lady Gaga's Little Monsters, Justin Bieber's Beliebers or ARMY for BTS fans – I would be lying if I said I didn't have to look some of these up! Eek! – but that doesn't mean that they don't have collective similarities with other fans and fandoms outside of their own. It's all pop culture after all!

- *Fangirls: Scenes from Modern Music Culture* by Hannah Ewens
- *Popular Music Fandom: Identities, Roles and Practices* by Mark Duffett
- *Emo: How Fans Defined a Subculture* by Judith May Fathallah

Now that is all squared away and owned up to, I think it's time for you and I to go on an adventure…

QUESTION

WHEN?

A Holmesian Problem

> 'A few words may suffice to tell the little that remains. An examination by experts leaves little doubt that a personal contest between the two men ended, as it could hardly fail to end in such a situation, in their reeling over, locked in each other's arms. Any attempt at recovering the bodies was absolutely hopeless, and there, deep down in that dreadful cauldron of swirling water and seething foam, will lie for all time the most dangerous criminal and the foremost champion of the law of their generation.'
>
> *The Final Problem*, Arthur Conan Doyle

We all know this, the death of Sherlock Holmes and Professor Moriarty, two men fighting on a waterfall and disappearing over the edge to vanish in the dark torrents below. Even if you haven't read the book, this moment has become something in our social consciousness. And it certainly is dramatic, but would it have been such a moment had it not been for the miraculous resurrection of this foremost champion of the law a over half a decade later? Well, unfortunately I do not have a window into another historical timeline so I can't tell you for sure, but I don't think it would be unfair to say that it is very possible.

Famously, Conan Doyle struggled with the fact that his most famous creation was not his most serious work, and made this attempt to kill him off in order to move onto those things that he perceived as a greater use of his time, but it was not to be. There's always a but with these things isn't there? Just ruining the end of a sentence, forcing away the final full stop. And in this instance, it was a case of the fans keeping the world's most famous detective from remaining at rest.

Fans? In the late nineteenth and early twentieth century? Before the internet? More likely than you'd think.

Around this period, there was a spike of interest in real life criminal investigation stories – true crime will, ironically, never die – driven by the newly-established detective branch of the police and the growing number of crime-solving technologies that came with them. The populous was clamouring for more, desperate to be the best arm-chair detective, and authors stepped up the fill the gap. But it would seem that with a willing market of readers came other, unforeseen issues for our most famous of detective writers.

When Conan Doyle sent Sherlock Holmes over the edge to his rather wet demise, there was uproar. People just couldn't believe it. Holmes? Gone? No more stories? No more mysteries? No more homoerotic tension – okay, so no one was saying that last one out loud, but I have met an awful lot of Sherlock Holmes fans and there is no way that somebody at the time wasn't thinking that. Just don't get me started on *Raffles*. This just wasn't okay. People took to the streets in black armbands, mourning his death *en masse*. Huge, public displays of grief poured out in honour of this fictional character. Letters were written. Oh yes, letters were written. It's a wonder that Conan Doyle ever managed to get through his post or read a newspaper again, all things considered.

The Sherlockians or Holmesians, as they are still known, let it be known how they felt about this greatest of tragedies. They put Conan Doyle in a vice of fandom-based pressure, long before *Justice League* fans demanded the Snyder Cut or Twitter exploded with fans rallying for a second series of *Of Our Flag Means Death*, and they won. Not only did they win, the pressure of the fanbase caused Conan Doyle to write one of the most famous pieces of detective fiction of all time, *The Hound of the Baskervilles*, before fully returning Holmes from the grave with *The Adventure of the Empty House* in 1903.

So, is it fair to say that without fans there would not have been half the canon of Sherlock Holmes that we now have? Reasonably, yes. Conan Doyle went on to write thirty-three more stories that he may well never have come back to had there not been a concerted fandom effort to get him back to writing these most popular of books. Rightly or wrongly on the part of fans to force a creator's hand in such a way – and that is something that we really ought to talk about, later – it would have been a very different world without this fandom.

Thing is though, it's not just the world of literature that would have lost out, but very likely the world of fandom, that very thing that we are here exploring, may well not have been quite the same either. Though that non-existent, magic window of mine, there is a world where maybe we wouldn't recognise fan culture at all because the Sherlockians didn't play their part, because not only were they making these very loud efforts to get his attention, but they were also coming together in a way that we would recognise as fandom behaviour in private spaces as well.

At the death of Sherlock Holmes something new was born. Fans started to collaborate, playing what they called 'The Sherlockian Game', looking at the works of Conan Doyle as if they were the real deal; not simply imaginative works of fiction but Dr Watson's true reports of his friend, in a world where Sherlock Holmes could have shown up at the house of any subject of Victorian Britain in order to help them. They started to dream up new stories to add to the collection, new moments in the lives of Holmes and Watson: they started writing fanfiction.

In actuality, fanfiction for Holmes had started before he died, but it was this moment, the grief, the outpouring of love and upset, that properly set these stories on their way. Fans were sharing, discussing, creating together in a way that any fan of the twenty-first century would know, and that was over a hundred years ago. And it's hardly stopped since.

That's it then, case closed. Sherlock Holmes created fandom. Or Arthur Conan Doyle did? Or the readers of Sherlock Holmes and Arthur Conan Doyle did? Or did they just intensify pre-existing behaviours? It would be easier if we could tie this all up in a neat, little bow and pick the turn of the twentieth century as the start of all this, following back those clues like our dear super sleuth, but just because mass social movements around media consumption weren't so much a thing, doesn't mean that the seeds of them weren't being spread. You can't start a fire if there's nothing to burn, and the spark of the Sherlockian fandom fell on some more than ready kindling.

I fear, my dear readers, that the game is still afoot.

Fandom will, err...
Find a Way

1

Let's make it clear before we move on that fandom pre-about the 1890s/1900s was not called fandom, and what we might associate with mass fan moments are and were referred to as manias. What we are doing is looking back and drawing lines between what people were doing in the past and attaching our own words and behavioural understandings to them with the benefit of hindsight and societal growth. Would I put money on some of these people and moments being part of modern fandom today? Yes. Would I be certain of winning it back? Probably not. Nothing is completely cut and dry, but gosh, people in the past would have loved to get their fanfic on.

Take your pick of historical periods and undoubtedly there will be argument for fan behaviours just getting off the starting blocks. Or more in some cases: Medieval, Tudor, Georgian, Victorian, right up to modern day.

So yes, it's more than fair to say that the word 'fandom' is a modern invention in the grand scheme of things, being coined in the last few years of the nineteenth century and coming fully into use in the twentieth, but that doesn't mean that what we might call fandom wasn't kicking about from well before that. As with many things, the giving of a word does tend to mean that the thing itself is becoming more noticeable, more mainstream if you like, and it is very clear that fandom found its strength in this period.

This was the home straight into what we know today, but that doesn't mean that it suddenly jumped out of the ground in the way of the dwarves of Middle Earth, or so the belief of many goes. Perhaps it might be better to think of a geyser, bubbling and building just under the ground. All it takes is the right conditions and what is waiting below the surface will find its time to explode onto the scene. So grab your ponchos and get ready to be in the splash zone, we're going to find out what caused this fandom bubble to burst.

Author note: For the sake of the word count, and the editor, this will very much be a passing look. A shame, indeed. However, if you wish to do further reading on the subject, to the back of the book with you. Enjoy!

Fanfiction? Are you there?

When you go right back, the idea of what is fan culture gets a bit muddled. Really quite muddled. Or, in fact, a lot muddled.

It's not that it's not there, or should it be that it's not that behaviours that resemble it aren't there, it's just that there is a feeling that what we can call 'fandom' or 'fan culture' is something that is attached to modern ideas of media. It simply doesn't count if this behaviour is focused on religion or classics or folk tales. If you like Loki in the Marvel comics or movies, you're a fan, but if you like him in the Norse Sagas, you're much more highbrow than that. Except, if the only media you have to hand for some considerable amount of human existence is the sagas, myths, religious texts, and tales around the fire, then what do we call it when you have someone paint your face into an oil painting of your favourite saint?

Back in the mists of time, somebody stood up and yelled across a cave or some rudimentary dwelling 'That's not canon and you know it!' and stormed off in a huff, or something in that vein anyway. Then some major religion or way of thinking split down the middle and some rather nasty wars or political assassinations happened, because people read a story differently – yes, I have summed up all of human history in one very easy and nuance-lacking paragraph. Sorry historians, you're all out of a job.

Aren't we glad that these things come down to having to take a little break away from your Discord channel nowadays? Mostly. But we'll get to that later.

And it kept happening. Arguing about stories and the meanings of them; this character did this; no they did this; no you're wrong it means this actually, on and on and on. And yes, that is trivialising major religious and political schisms that caused centuries worth of war, trauma, and upheaval just a bit, but it does seem a touch familiar, don't you think? Twitter user 501AnakinLuvver – this is an entirely fictional handle and any bearing to real life people or persons is accidental – was not the first person to get all caught up in the meaning of a throwaway line of dialogue.

Okay, okay, this isn't 'fandom'. It's culture and society. It's important stuff, these are the stories that shape the world we live in, that gave us some sort of understanding of how the world works, looking for not just a reflection of ourselves but also wanting to see our world view reflected in those stories. It's rather a large part of any given person that they see the world around them in a slightly different way to others and feel the need to prove their version right, be that part of fandom or as a part of society, and it just so happens that when your society is based on stories, the changing of them and all the arguments that happen around them impact the world more than they do when you have huge amounts of media that is external to that.

Even then, unless you were in a seat of power, or looking to take said seat of power, it didn't much matter how you saw the stories. For the most part, how much you changed them to fit your way of looking at the world was for each group that came into contact with them. People were making it fit their understanding, to match what they saw every day, to make what seemed so distant relatable. It's hard to find meaning in legends if you can't see yourself in them.

It was the job of players and storytellers to make the stories fit the situation, so they changed each myth they told depending on the people in front of them and the place they were telling it in. Oral storytelling traditions meant that no single version of canon existed, everyone had their own one, just for them. They might change the ending, the characters' appearances, the country it was set in, the names, or all of the above to the point that it wasn't really the original story at all.

And then they might publish it, called *Fifty Shades of Grey* and it was never a *Twilight* AU fanfiction.

A little silly, sure, but you get the point. What we would call fanfiction was just the normal way of storytelling; you dropped the characters into your Celtic village AU (Alternative Universe) out of their original setting and called them Woden instead of Oden and it's a whole new myth, right? That's what the Romans did with the Greeks and they did pretty well out of that.

It's not until things get set down in stone, or on paper, that this chopping and changing of stories really becomes an issue. If you can't point to an 'original' telling and say that's how it goes you can't argue for canon, and even then, if most people can't read, then only certain people are going to be arguing that anyway, while everyone else just adds their own changes and endings and circumstances to the plot as they tell them.

You can see it all throughout history, and it's also worth noting that what we might call fan behaviour, particularly that around fanfiction and fanart, was, in the past, often seen to be a way to add legitimacy to a new work of your own by linking it to another. It's not just religious or mythical stories that get this treatment, though they are the main focus of it. The case of what might be one of the easiest 'self-insert' fanfiction is a version of *The Canterbury Tales* rewritten by a man called John Lidgate in which he put himself in as one of the pilgrims with his own tale within the narrative.

Plenty of modern media is still doing this. DC and Marvel both have sets of characters that link in with the myths and legends of the ancient world in order to give a level of credibility and believability to the world of superheroes. Superman might be an alien, but Wonder Woman is an Amazon and the daughter of any number of Greek gods depending on the canon of that particular story. By borrowing from something that is well known in the social consciousness, and which already explains something about the world building you are doing, the characters gain an extra dimension to them without any effort.

The same is true of how paintings of religious or mythical scenes feature the clothing and locations of the time and place they were created in. There's a level of aiming to legitimise the painter and the patron as well as make the work relatable, a sort of 'well of course I'm special, look at how well placed I am near to Christ'. Total Mary-Sue behaviour. One could go so far to say that this isn't that different from getting your photo with your fav at a convention or at Disneyland. You're showing your credibility as a fan to other fans, and signposting that you're in the club. You're special.

To quote Media and Cinema Studies professor, Paul Booth, who has written more than a little bit on the subject, and who I was far too excited to talk to while I was researching this book – I geek out over fandom academics, what did you expect from someone writing this book?

> '[T]he ultimate human condition is to experience in-ephemeral emotion about something. It is, in many ways, what separates us from, from other beings on our planet. That, that we can conceptualise the fact that we're having emotions. I think, you know, I've got this new dog, and this dog is super happy all the time. He doesn't know that he's happy. He just is. We have this ability to step out of ourselves and to say, I recognise that I am happy, and it is because of this thing. And that that's happened since the beginning of humankind. We call it fandom today. But it has gone by many different guises.'

Thanks, Paul! We'll see you later.

So yes, it's muddled, you could go so far as to say that it's murky. Really murky. What is and isn't 'fan' behaviour pretty much depends on how you are looking at fans and fandom as a whole, because the behaviours themselves, the self-insertion, the changing of stories to fit your alternative telling, the art, the discussion, everything, it's all there, it's just not quite it yet. But as shocking as it might be, it's very possible humans have always been humans, and those of us today just have the benefit of compounded knowledge.

The Shakespeare Jubilee of 1769

Shakespeare Con 1769! Get your commemorative doublets and carved memorabilia from the tree that inspired the bard now! And don't forget to show off your best cosplays while you're at it: we all can't wait to see the best Falstaff and Lady MacBeth of this year's event. The pop culture event of the year, brought to you by celebrated actor David Garrick!

Alright, this might be a bit silly but it's not as far off reality as you might think. In 1769 David Garrick, known as the most distinguished actor of his generation and for his love of all things Shakespeare, set up The Shakespeare Jubilee. Originally planned to celebrate the opening of Stratford-Upon-Avon's new town hall, alongside the unveiling of a statue of the bard that Garrick had donated to the town, it spilled out into a three day festival, including a ball, a 'grand pageant', performances of music, singing and sonnets, as well as a fireworks display and a Garrick himself performing 'An Ode to Shakespeare'.

There was even an opening ceremony, that came with all the pomp that you might associate with these sorts of things. Garrick was named the 'first Steward of the Jubilee' and presented with a medallion and wand carved from the mulberry tree outside of Shakespeare's birthplace.

Author note: conventions have always been a strange mix between deeply nerdy and a secret society of some sort, there's always a guy with a wand somewhere and you're never quite sure if he's meant to be in charge or not.

Up until this point, the home of Shakespeare hadn't been the mass tourist attraction that it would become in later decades, but the Jubilee saw people from all over the country flock into the small market town. The place was barely able to cope with flood of Shakespeare fanatics, let alone their desire for Shakespeare-themed events, paraphernalia and general knick-knacks – who doesn't want a medal and ribbon with the face of William Shakespeare on it?!

It just wasn't the sort of thing that happened to little towns in eighteenth-century England.

If you've ever been to a convention, you'll have some understanding of what it is to be amidst the throng of fans, clamouring to get to the first panel of the day, or to get the excusive piece of merchandise, but this probably came as a bit of a surprise to the denizens of Stratford. Particularly when the heavens opened on the second day and the grand pageant, along with the 200 costumed guests and other fans there to take part were suddenly without anywhere to be.

The grand pageant appears to have been the Shakespeare Jubilee's predecessor to the cosplay masquerade of today in the style of a carnival procession that was to parade through Stratford, followed by Garrick's performance in a Rotunda specially erected for the Jubilee and finished off with a masquerade ball and fireworks, but the rain stopped play. It's still pretty hard to cope with for a seasoned visitor of these events nowadays and modern events tend to be protected from the elements.

The Rotunda, along with hand painted scenery screens that were hung throughout the town in order to evoke the feelings of the theatre, were badly damaged, and some of the visitors were hurt when parts of the Rotunda, including seating, collapsed after Garrick's performance. But never say that fans will be washed out so easily. The masquerade ball went ahead, despite the rising water levels in the river outside, and it was reported that all were in high spirits. If you have ever had the joy to attend the New Year's parade in London, you will know it takes more than adverse weather to stop cosplayers, and that seems to have always been the case.

Unfortunately, unless you had a ticket, you weren't getting into many, or actually most, of the events that were programmed, but that didn't stop people showing up. Just like today, plenty of folks felt like chancing their arm at getting in free, or simply wanted to see the sights, but with the only two free activities – the grand pageant and the fireworks – turning out to be, by all accounts a bit of a wash out, the whole thing ended up as bit of a joke.

Widely mocked by critics and Garrick's own contemporaries at the time, the Shakespeare Jubilee failed to take off as the world's first fan convention. However, it was able to be used as a starting point for a campaign to save Shakespeare's birthplace in later years and very much put Stratford-Upon-Avon at the centre of the world for any good lover of the bard. It has become a place of fandom pilgrimage with parts of the original Jubilee still included in the celebrations.

What stands out about the Shakespeare festival, is how similar it feels to modern conventions, meets and fan events that take place today, right down to printed handbills of the programme and pop-up sellers all flogging merch you really don't need but you'll get because it's part of the fun – you know the stall, you know you do. Live performances of podcasts, or music artists playing at conventions is much the same as the Drury Lane band playing in Garrick's Rotunda, and folks will definitely queue in the rain and worse to see it. Fans just can't help being fans it would seem.

But it also has that ring of people going 'this is a bit strange' and 'why do you want to play pretend', that rings true today. Many saw it as more about Garrick than Shakespeare. One critic, Charles Dibdin, wrote:

> '...the whole business was concerted to levy contributions on his [Garrick's] friends, retainers, dependants, and the public in general, for no other motive upon earth than to fill his own pockets... The tomb of Shakespeare was stript of laurels to adorn the brow of Garrick.'

Which is not entirely unfair, and most definitely a critique that has been levelled at many a fan over the centuries. You could probably log on to Twitter right now and see someone saying exactly that about Stephen Moffat, *Doctor Who* fan and series creator, or *Star Wars* director and super fan Jon Favreau. Fame and fandom can become an odd and traitorous mix to navigate at times, especially with the eyes of other fans upon you, but we'll get to that.

With the Jubilee, people simply didn't get it. Particularly why someone as celebrated as Garrick and the many other successful and well-to-do guests, would want to attend something that would make them seem stupid. But this was an event for fans, by fans. Even if they weren't calling themselves that, these were people coming together to celebrate something they had a shared love for with nothing but joy; wind, rain and flooding be damned.

In fact, a group called The Shakespeare Ladies Club had been instrumental in the Jubilee happening, just as much as Garrick. They had been a large part of bringing Shakespeare back into popularity during the period, petitioning theatres to put on productions of his plays when they were very much out of fashion with the theatre-going public. The Club had raised funds for the statue at Poet's Corner, that Garrick unveiled as part of proceedings, and the Jubilee itself. In short, they were a fan club and, much like the Holmesian clubs that would come later, can be credited with a large part of the work around Shakespeare becoming as pop-culturally important as he is, with writers and critics of their day lauding them as the champions of the bard.

And The Shakespeare Ladies Club was not alone. Groups like this, and others, were about to start being seen everywhere, discussion was the talk of the town.

Being able to sit and chat, take in the news, the gossips, the ideas of the time and be there when it was all happening at once, that was going to push what being a creator and what being a fan meant to new levels.

Be Part of the Discussion

One of things that you really need to know about the eighteenth century is that folks really liked a discussion group and a space in which to do it. Everyone was getting their enlightenment on, and all the best and brightest minds were finding themselves in salons, coffee houses and clubs, talking politics, philosophy and art. And a lot more besides. The creators of ideas were mixed in amongst those who were fans of their work, or the works themselves were being born out of the creative collaboration and general maelstrom of ideas that was bouncing around inside these spaces. Honestly, we have a lot to thank coffee for besides a population of caffeine addicts.

A lot of these spaces were inhabited by wealthy or up-and-coming men, making their waves on the world in one way or another. They were, for the most part, the educated elite, and they were always desperate for more news, bigger ideas, and what was going to be the next big thing.

Admirers would have direct access to the orators/artists/poets/creative profession of choice in these public salons and would also be encouraged by their fellow patrons to attend the new popular thing or try out the next shining star's work. It was a bit like Twitter of the 1700s but with more fancy nibbles and less dog pilling – at least I hope so, it would be even worse in person!

That being said, popular culture was certainly not limited to the wealthy and educated. Anyone who could afford it could go to see theatre (and it wasn't just Shakespeare), speakers or music in pubs and later music halls, with wild excitement, the very picture of those Beatles fans at the front of the crowd, but with more body fluids – don't ask, but do check the reading list.

Unfortunately, a lot of the elements of fandom that revolved around fanworks weren't always available to those who were illiterate, or at least we don't know that much about them as their discussions and ideas simply weren't recorded in ways that they might have been for others.

However, we do know a lot about one group of people who were very much doing the fan thing and who weren't wealthy, educated men, but wealthy, educated women. Women who had access to education in whatever way in this period took a lot of pleasure in communicating their enjoyment of the media and topics of the day in many ways, some more unusual than others.

Now, I told myself I wasn't going to go down the Lord Byron path, he's had his ego stroked enough already and he's dead, but his fans are something of a wonder. The way that his fans (often women) reacted to him and engaged with fan culture surrounding him was more of a form of self-expression, using his works and the perception of this dark, brooding hero as a catalyst to explore their own ideas and desires.

In a time when women had very few outlets in which to explore their own sexuality, let alone express it, these fan letters, many of which are anonymous, show that whatever Byron was doing was being responded to in a way that we would definitely recognise today as fannish behaviour. These are ye olde thirst tweets.

There's even an argument that could be made for some of these being self-insert fanfic since a good few are written in Byronic verse, mimicking or replying to his poems with their own ideas. It doesn't take long for the 'Byronic hero' to make its way into common culture as we see the cultivated, public persona of the poet enter into popular fiction. Heathcliff remind you of anyone? Or Mr Rochester perhaps?

By 1831, The Brontë siblings had already got a body of fanfic-esque work under their belt with what is now called *The Brontë Juvenilia*. This was a series of fantasy stories, set in their own fictional world – Glass Town, Angria, and Gondal – but used real characters, such as the Duke of Wellington and Napoleon Bonaparte. The stories revolved around the various adventures of these characters, including riding on dragons, with all four of the children adding to the stories in interconnecting ways.

It's not really a surprise that these siblings, who came from an isolated lifestyle, looked to the world around them and fictionalised it in one way or another. They did what all those people down the years did, they made stories to explore their understanding of the world and to make it fantastic. Perhaps even inserted themselves into those fantasies. Fanfiction or not, there is nothing wrong with filing off the serial numbers of what you know and making something new.

What the Dickens!

Celebrity and all that comes with it was becoming more and more a part of life throughout the eighteenth and early nineteenth centuries, but as the industrial revolution marched steadily nearer, the void between creator, their works and their fans was becoming steadily vaster. Long gone were the days of sitting around, discussing the next playwright or actress to come on the scene surrounded by all the up-and-coming of the day; creators were finding it harder and harder to stop admirers making journeys to their homes, or traipsing through the gardens in order to catch a glimpse of the object of their adoration, something that modern celebs and creators have very high walls and scary looking security guards to help with.

Fans were becoming a much bigger part of life than anyone would have guessed. Why were people hiding out in bushes in order to see a writer cross their lawn, or using a pilgrimage to someone's writing nook as a holiday.

This is not new. Obviously. Pilgrimage in particular has been happening since there were places to go pilgrim to. Mostly this was for religious purposes, but the more people and media became popular culture in their own right, the more admirers wanted to go to the places the objects of their admiration were attached too. Byron and Shelley famously went on pilgrimage around Europe to visit the homes of those who had inspired them, with people then following in their footsteps because Byron and Shelley had done it. Very meta that. But as is often the case with fans, and I say this with the best will in the world, sometimes things went a little far. The constant attention, letters from fans, seeing people watching them and feeling the constant need to be producing drove many creators and celebrities to distraction.

In order to allow fans access to them, some creators started to put on touring shows of them reading from their novels or showing a play of their works with a talk, allowing both admirer and admired a give-and-take from the situation. The take, well it made a nice monetary advance on any works that were on their way. Fans have always been willing to spend on fandom.

Whether the reasoning was money, safety or a desire for appreciation from their fanbases, tours where very popular, especially in America.

Charles Dickens was one of the biggest names to tour the States, and he did it twice. Though the second time was less of a success, due to him dying.

Dickens was one of the biggest writers of his age, a man who sold out theatres on tour and with theatrical versions of his own books, who knew how to market himself and is credited with inventing Christmas, and so adored that he could not walk down the streets without being recognised. He, as many before and since, struggled with it, but he also knew his audience. He had a sturdy fanbase, and a classy niche of Christmas novels alongside his other works, that he could rely on. That wasn't something to be sniffed at.

He would schedule his books to be released at the same time as a stage production of said book in order to open up as many avenues as possible for his fanbase to interact with the works. This might also include serialised versions of stories instead of a book release straight away, or a reading tour at Christmas. He was a savvy marketer and saw the advantageous nature of having a prominent fandom around you.

And he wasn't the only one. Oscar Wilde toured not only his plays but also as a public speaker, being well known and admired for his wit before his plays and prose even took off in any major way. Tours allowed you to build your reputation, be seen by new audiences, or create a storm around you available to the fans in a way that you weren't as a creator through only owning a book. People could buy merchandise, collect photographic images, or perhaps get a signature to share with friends. It really was the equivalent of BTS coming to town when Dickens or Wilde rolled up on tour.

Where in the past fans had access to the creators in public spaces, now they were beginning to held at arms-length in order to put a barrier between creator, work and fans. This meant that fans, particularly women, had to create ways of interacting with their favourite celebrities or creators, to show their fan credentials as well as connect with others in their community. Hard to do when a lot of the time you're stuck inside waiting to be called on or going out to do the calling.

Many middle- and upper-class women were very taken with the new style of fan culture around this time. Though the usage of the word 'fan' is still a few years off, it is in the nineteenth century that the true hallmarks of modern fan culture are born. Many of these women started to collect photographs of famous or influential people, keeping them in albums or commonplace books; a sort of journal that you would share with friends to write comments to each other or your own thoughts on a subject, draw or paint images and obviously show your collections to each other. It was rather like a Tumblr dashboard – and about the same level of fannish behaviour was involved in commonplace books as on Tumblr. You just know these Victorian fans would squee – documenting how you felt about a new poem, or placing a prized photograph in it for others to see but only those who shared your interests. Social media pre-the internet age.

Of course, these collections were wildly mocked by men at the time, calling them frivolous and ridiculous ways to spend your time. But fans have always pushed on despite criticism, and commonplace books grew in popularity up until the end of the nineteenth century and technology started to overtake the need.

THE DEATH OF SHERLOCK HOLMES.

Front Piece from *The Memoirs of Sherlock Holmes* 1894 – Special Collections Toronto Public Library.

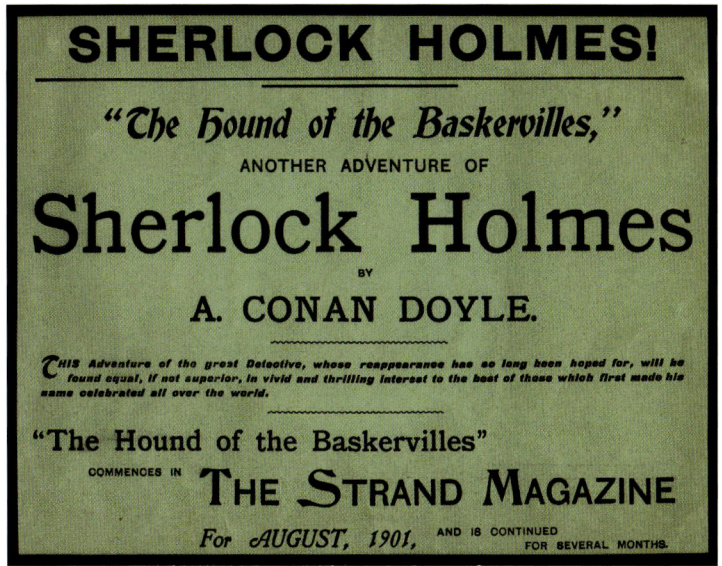

SHERLOCK HOLMES!
"The Hound of the Baskervilles,"
ANOTHER ADVENTURE OF
Sherlock Holmes
BY
A. CONAN DOYLE.
THIS Adventure of the great Detective, whose reappearance has so long been hoped for, will be found equal, if not superior, in vivid and thrilling interest to the best of those which first made his name celebrated all over the world.
"The Hound of the Baskervilles"
COMMENCES IN
THE STRAND MAGAZINE
For AUGUST, 1901,
AND IS CONTINUED FOR SEVERAL MONTHS.

Hound of the Baskervilles Strand broadsheet – Special Collections Toronto Public Library.

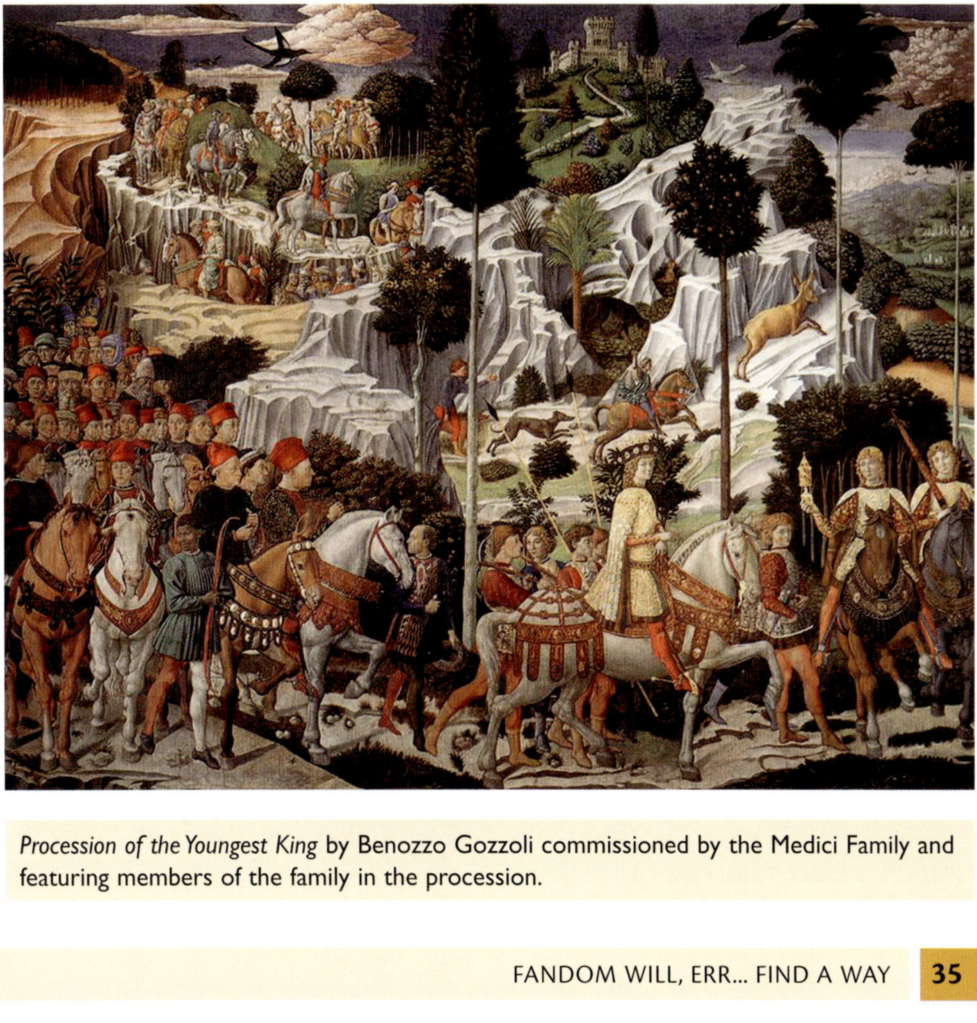

Procession of the Youngest King by Benozzo Gozzoli commissioned by the Medici Family and featuring members of the family in the procession.

Illustrated page of Chaucer's *Canterbury Tales*.

Right: Narcissus by Caravaggio, an example of mythological stories in classical art.

Below: David Garrick performing his *Ode To Shakespeare* in the Rotunda.

Mr. Garrick reciting the Ode, in honor of Shakespeare, at the Jubilee at Stratford; with the Musical Performers, &c.

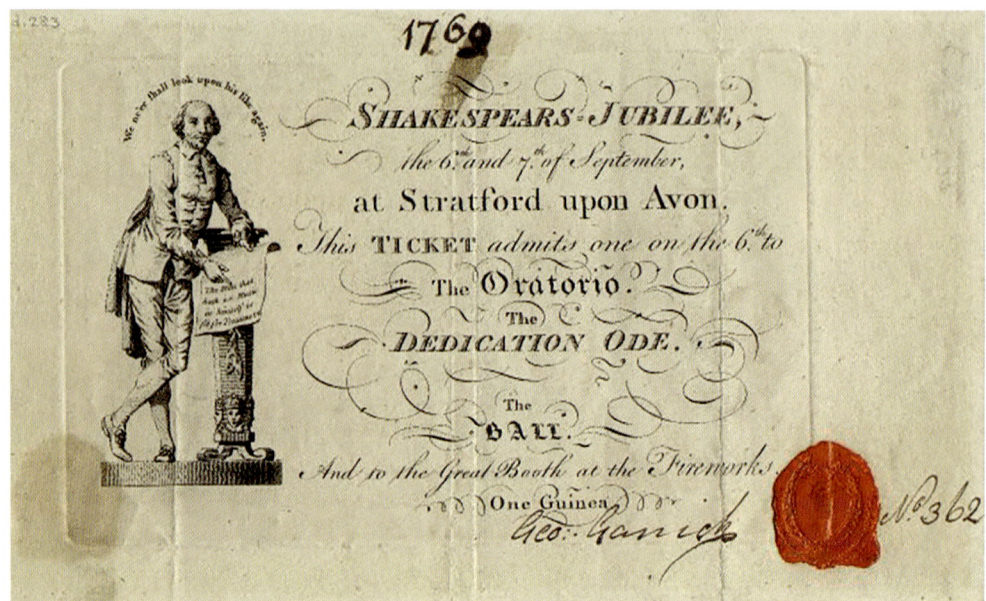

A Ticket To Shakespeare's Jubilee signed by George Garrick – This image was originally posted to Flickr by Folger Shakespeare Library.

Interior of a London coffee house in the seventeenth century.

George Gordon Byron, Sixth Baron Byron, by Richard Westall, National Portrait Gallery.

The Brontë Sisters by Patrick Branwell.

The Future is Now: Moving into the Twentieth Century

2

What happens when you mix explosive technology with growing education across populations and brand-new types of media that are responding to that just as fast, if not faster than, the world this is happening in? That's right, we've hit crunch time. At the beginning of the twentieth century, fans are born, for realsies this time.

The word 'fan' comes into use in 1899, used to describe the crowds cheering for their team at a Kansas City baseball match, but quickly became attached to supporters of all types of sport and popular media. And what a lot of new media there was. Folks were crowding in to see movies and newsreels, the wireless could beam plays and music straight into your home and the price of printing was so cheap new magazines and newspapers were popping up all over the place.

This is not to say that the turn of the twentieth century was a beautiful moment when everyone got to go to school, put their hands on all this new technology, and suddenly we could all be fans of things, no not all. It was, as with anyone being able to go the theatre in the Tudor era, or the introduction of mass-produced newspapers and cheap printing in the eighteenth and nineteenth centuries, adding a level of accessibility in a way that was never the case before. It opened up the world of popular entertainment not just to new audiences, but to new spaces.

The change from entertainment being purely in public spaces and into the home, or your neighbours' home, allowed people to engage with media differently. You no longer had to go to the pub or the music hall to hear the latest songs, or see this week's slice of melodrama, now it was beamed right into your kitchen, wirelessly. You could be listening to the BBC Light Programme in your kitchen at midday and still go out to the theatre for your evening entertainment.

And someone had to feed this need for content. With more spaces to fill, literally, more people were stepping up to the plate to create the media that the audiences were demanding, people who would never have had that opportunity just decades before. This easy, well easier, movement into creative media, for those outside of the upper classes, led to a wave of exciting new ideas hitting the mainstream.

This change in accessibility on both sides of the fan space is a massive part of why fandom is what it is now, and why it had to grow out of behaviours from other things. You can't like something you don't know about, so you can't have mass social fan communities, but what happens when everyone can know about something? Perhaps a serialised group of stories in *The Strand Magazine* about a detective and his doctor buddy? Or even better, stories that reflect this brave, new world that was shaping up?

Alongside this technological boom in reality, the popular new genre of science fiction was finding its way onto the bookshelves and magazine racks as cheap, affordable paperbacks, sprouting interest in subjects that many had never had access to before. A fast-changing world was not only creating access but responding to it with new media and tales of where we were heading.

So, what happens when all this gets mixed together? Because it feels like the powder keg of fandom is waiting to happen.

Fanclubs, Fanclubs, Fanclubs!

I have a bit of a soft spot for early twentieth century fans. There's something quite romantic about all sitting around in a village hall, or someone's flat, putting together your monthly issue of Sci-Fi South West club magazine, called something like '*Zapps!*' or '*Journeys into Tomorrow*' while someone discusses the finer points of Weird Fiction in the corner. It all gains that noir fiction vibe, the place wreathed in cigarette smoke and full of the sound of a typewriter. It's all so cool and mysterious, in a rather quirky way granted, but maybe its just me.

This might be a touch on the fictional side but the fanclubs and communities of the 1920s and '30s were out there holding meetings, debating the newest works to come out of the exiting, new genre of science-fiction, printing their own publications and circulating them nation-wide. Many had multiple branches that talked to each other through their magazines or 'zines' and met up in person a few times a year in larger scale gatherings that grew the social and fannish connections even further.

Science, or speculative, fiction was at the heart of these clubs. As with detective fiction some 50 years prior, people wanted to discuss the technological ideas that were being thrown up by the genre and explore the possibilities of some truth being held in the fictional stories, the old moniker of science-fiction being a prelude to science fact very much being born in these clubs.

It also turns out that science-fiction is a prelude to a lot more science-fiction, as being given a space to explore ideas didn't just encourage people to look into making these ideas a reality but also how to make wilder and wider ideas as well, which were all published within the community 'zines.

It's around this time that we see the term 'fanfiction' first being used, but as much it would have been cool to have seen the *War of the Worlds* coffee shop AU, this isn't quite the same fanfiction as we would know today. Instead it referred to fans writing fiction in the genre of their fanclub 'zine of choice. Some of the most famous science-fiction, fantasy and pulp-fiction writers came out of this style of fanfiction, including Isaac Asimov and the infamous H.P. Lovecraft amongst a myriad of others.

A lot of these fanclubs were popular with the growing population of students and academics as well as the new generation of young professionals that were coming into the work force. In a post-industrial revolution world, more people from different areas of life were taking up white collar jobs instead of factory or manual jobs as they would have in the past, and there were finding themselves able to access higher levels of education. What that meant in reality was that many fanclubs were predominantly spaces for young, mostly white, men. Few women or minorities were able to become part of the clubs for various reasons, this being the 1920s/30s you can guess a few pretty easily, but some, such as the acclaimed 'mother of cosplay' Myrtle R. Douglas, did make their presence known and were a boon to the way that these clubs developed.

Fandom really wouldn't be the same without them no matter how other worldly they might feel to today. That being said, these types of clubs haven't disappeared, they just don't tend to be so hasty about these things anymore, baa-rum!

The Tolkien Society: Taking it Seriously

It's hard to say it, but how seriously do people take media studies? Let alone fan studies? For a lot of people it might feel like a bit of a joke; it definitely was when I was at school, much to my shame, which is just strange considering that we live in a world that is practically controlled by the media we take in and the way we react to it. Studying media is super helpful, and many of the fans of same media have recognised that over the decades setting up fanclubs that go beyond getting a newsletter once a month and early access tickets to a world tour.

One such group, was the Tolkien Society, set up to celebrate, study and promote the works of J.R.R.Tolkien. With Tolkien coming from an academic background himself it made sense that an academic focus should be applied to being a fan, so many began to study his works as they would the historical texts and sagas that he drew from when writing *The Lord of the Rings* and the other books set in Middle-Earth.

Fan communities like this were often very analytical and took it all very seriously, debating, discussing, etc and wanted what they were doing to be seen as a credible form of literary and artistic discussion, since a lot of the mainstream in this area did not take sci-fi and fantasy all that seriously (they often are still very dismissive of 'genre fiction'). What this did was add a certain legitimacy to the fanworks that were created and by extension to the fans themselves. Much in the same way as the storytellers and scholars of the past took validation for their works by linking them to myths, legends and religious stories, so did these fans.

It feels like a rather excellent coincidence that this behaviour is mirrored in fans of Tolkien's works, with him basing them on the very same sagas and folklore that lent that validity all that time ago.

The Tolkien Society was, or is, far from being the only group of this type though it is almost a 'buzzword' for this style of fan community. On top of that it has been a mainstay of fan culture since its conception and is still running events, a regularly updated website, its own awards ceremonies, and publishes its own journal of papers. It is hard not to consider The Tolkien Society a major part of the world of fandom, as well as of Tolkien, to this day.

World Con

Conventions come and go, fandoms rise and fall, but World Con always remains. It's the longest, continually running, convention in the world, starting in 1939. Okay, so it's not entirely continually running but you can hardly blame them for a world war shutting it down for a few years. That aside, it has been going for just shy of a century, moving from country to country, city to city, bringing sci-fi joy and nerdiness to us all.

I have, on one occasion, been able to attend World Con in person, and it does not disappoint, even when you can get to a comic con every weekend a year if you want to. It stands out in what it provides as an event and the way that it works. It is definitely an ancient beast all of its own, walking through fandom as a giant of fan culture.

But it can't quite lay claim to being the first. That goes to a British science-fiction convention in 1937, to which 20 people showed up. But one of those people was Arthur C. Clarke so, small it may have been, but mighty it still was.

Fan meets before had been more like little markets, sell-and-swap type things, often with rows of boxes on tables and little else, or discussion-based fanclub meetings as mentioned before, that may have had bigger meetings of different branches. World Con sought to expand on that and grow it into a bigger space (literally) and bring together people from different fan spheres but who all had a similar point of interest around sci-fi and fantasy in general.

They had a guest of honour, the first being Frank R. Paul a pulp magazine illustrator and specialist in sci-fi artworks, alongside other participants such as author Ray Bradbury and rocket scientist John D. Clark. There were also panels and talks, and the whole thing was themed as 'The World of Tomorrow'; it really must have been something for those who travelled from their small fan communities to this major, fandom experience.

It definitely sat in the realms of the scholarly, and continues to do so. But alongside all the more academic panels that were held, World Con was also the first place we saw cosplay appearing on the fandom scene in a big way. It's hard to pinpoint the first cosplay, much in the same way as it is hard to say when fan culture really started, and there are plenty of candidates for the position, including an alien from Mars and science-fiction book signing both around the turn of the century. What we can know is that this was the first time costumes were recorded at a fan event – though as with any 'academia', I am waiting excitedly to be proved wrong.

Myrtle R. Douglas, aka MoRoJo, showed up in a self-designed cosplay at that she, and her then partner Forry Accaman, wore around the convention hall. A lot of people were so not chill about it, seeing it as not taking the convention seriously, but, the costumes caught on in a massive way. MoRoJo's concept of fan-costuming developed one of the most interesting parts of fandom culture.

Personally, I see the moment of MoRoJo showing up in cosplay – then called future fashion or hero costuming – as a point in which another way of being a fan in fan spaces was suddenly allowed. It was a very different way to celebrate media and be a fan that people didn't think was respectful, and that shook things up in the best way possible!

This along with original fiction are the precursors to the way that the more transformative elements of fandom are today, moving away from a strictly academic viewpoint and creating, well, a creative version of that fan enjoyment. There is a huge amount of different ways to be a fan, and this moment opened up that door that bit wider to start seeing that.

What all of these fanclubs, meetings, conventions and works made clear though was that science-fiction, and its fans, were here to stay. This is was a brave new world of storytelling coming into its own, celebrated and championed by a community of like-minded individuals who wanted to push the boundaries of how they could tell these stories and who they could tell them to.

Right: Forry Ackerman and MoRoJo at World Con in New York 1939.

Below left: *Weird Tales* cover 1925 from the Popular Fiction Publishing Co.

Below right: *Weird Tales* cover 1935 from the Popular Fiction Publishing Co.

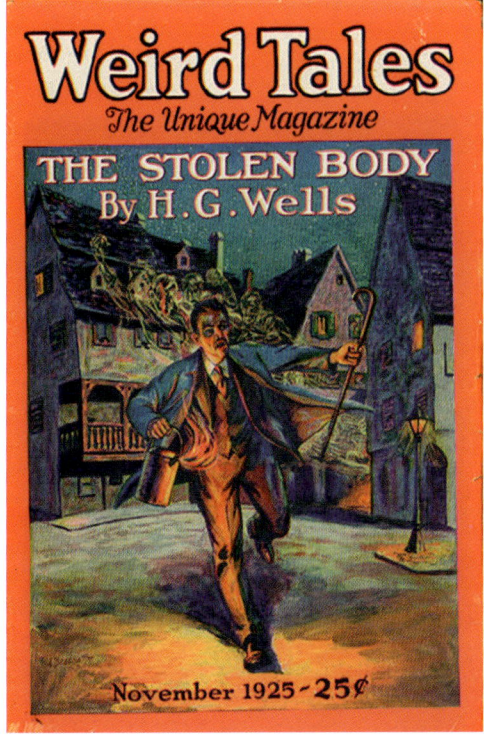

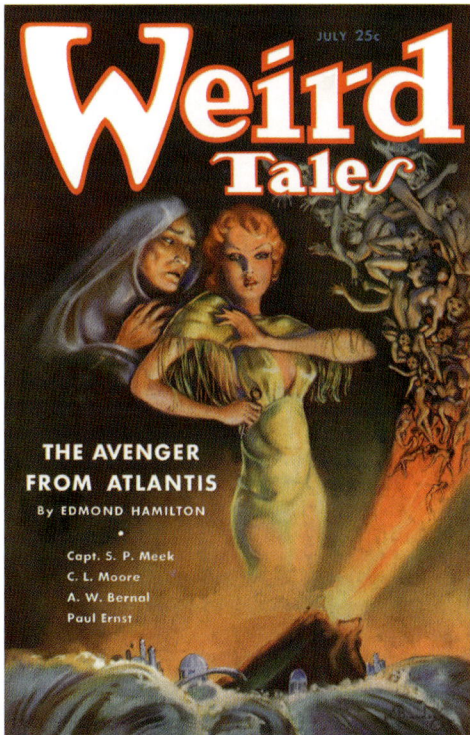

Left: *Weird Tales* cover 1940 from the Popular Fiction Publishing Co.

Below: Line-up for fancy dress at World Con 65.

Dressing up at World Con 65.

Left: William Hartnell as The First Doctor in 1963.

Below: The Doctor and companions, Susan, Ian and Barbara, 1963.

The Doctor with his new companions, Vicki and Steven, in 1965.

A letter of complaint about *Doctor Who* to the *Radio Times* in 1966.

The Three Doctors, Jon Pertwee, Patrick Troughton and William Hartnell.

3 To Go Where No Fan Has Gone Before

At 3:30am on 18 June 1947 Pan Am Flight 121 crashed near the Euphrates River, killing eight passengers and seven crew. An engine failure mid-flight, which caused a fuel leak, leading to the second engine catching fire, sent the plane plummeting to Earth despite the efforts of the captain and crew to stop it.

Only one officer survived, having been in the main cabin, supporting the passengers as best he could, during the flight. He took charge. Despite his own injuries, he, and the surviving crew dragged as many passengers as they could from the wreckage, in the face of fire spreading throughout the plane and the insecure nature of the plane's hull, risking their own safety to evacuate the craft. The name of this officer was Gene Roddenberry, a World War Two veteran and eventually creator of the most popular science fiction show of all time; *Star Trek*.

Roddenberry put his creation of *Star Trek* and the ethical backbone at its heart down to this tragic misadventure aboard Pan Am Flight 121.

A lot of the tale of the crash, being stranded, and the subsequent rescue operation that Roddenberry told over the years is up for debate, and there was definitely elements of him fudging the narrative in order to fit the ideas of *Trek*, and the fanbase's expectations, if not a touch of self-aggrandising, but you can't blame a man for a good story.

The way Roddenberry tells it, the survivors did their best to rescue everyone and everything they could from the plane, which, miraculously, included first aid kits as well as some of the luggage. At some point after this, while they were setting up a camp, they were approached by nomads who had seen the plane crashing. Roddenberry says that he convinced the locals not to rob the group, rather to take from the crash site, through his charisma and wit, much in the manner of his famously charming Captain Kirk. Whatever else, he did manage to organise a search team to head out to find help.

With the worst injured remaining with a few to tend them and the supplies, Roddenberry and the rest went in search of a telegraph line that they had seen in the distance and knew must lead to a town one way or another. They split the group to follow it in each direction and to report back. It didn't take long. A settlement was spotted some four miles off and Roddenberry took it on himself to hike through the dunes to call in support.

He called at 8am, five hours after the crash.

Roddenberry later said that the survivors of the crash were instrumental in how he brought together the ideas of the crew of the *Enterprise*. The humanity of the situation, pulling together in dire straits and in an alien environment, can so clearly be seen reflected in *Star Trek* no matter what era you pick. This moment in Roddenberry's life became a baked-in part of the show's narrative, and that affected the fanbase just as much as the show.

Without the crash of Pan Am Flight 121 fandom would, categorically, not be what it is today, because *Trek* fans did fandom like no other. This is a fandom that would go where no fan had gone before.

Star Trekking

It is hard to argue against the idea that modern fandom would not be what it is without *Star Trek*. In particularly the fans that gathered around *Trek*, who were, more often than not, housewives.

When *Star Trek* hit screens a whole new world of fandom opened up, purely since it was on screens, small screens, in the home. This meant people, women for the most part, who had not had access to sci-fi fan clubs for literary works or possibly had just never encountered science fiction or fantasy literature before, and if they had didn't know that fan clubs for it existed – pre-internet you had better hope someone put something in the local paper or on a notice board or you'd be none the wiser! – suddenly had it on their TV screens to sit down and watch.

This is not to say that women were not in fandom before this. Of course they were, don't be silly, but it was a very closed circle that was harder for women to enter. Even with technology and all the progressive changes through the beginning of the twentieth century, being in fan spaces was still something that required a level of social privilege, education, money and time. TV changed that. It built on what the wireless had started, giving people that access to the wider world, without having to take large amounts of time out of their day-to-day lives to do it. But with a small selection of channels, this meant that everyone was going to be watching the same, and that is the kicker. You could all talk about what you were watching and people went mad for *Trek*.

The stories were literally out of this world, but the characters were people you could relate to, more importantly they were people EVERYONE could relate to. It wouldn't be a joke to say that a large part of the success of *Star Trek* was the diverse cast that people from all walks of life could see themselves in, and it was ground-breaking in doing this. That vision of Roddenberry's that came from his experiences as a pilot and a war veteran led him to wanting to push for a diverse, inclusive and peaceful version of the future and that meant showing it on screen.

Star Trek gave us a black woman as a main member of the cast who wasn't a servant or slave, and the first interracial kiss. There was a Russian man and a Japanese man as main characters at the height of the Cold War and not long after America had put Japanese people in internment camps and dropped nuclear bombs on Japanese cities. It pushed discussions of sexism and gender identity. It envisioned a future with peace and cooperation and equality at its heart.

It pushed so many boundaries, opened so many discussions and included so many people who would have never thought they'd see themselves represented in any media – of course it gained a following.

Star Trek, like every moment of increased and noticeable fan presence before it, hits on the key factor of bringing more people into the fan sphere, not just with more access to the thing itself but with increased communication about it as well. The more you could talk about a subject, theorise, deep dive or 'squee' about your favourite characters, the more you are going to become attached to it. If it's only you it's very hard to keep a motivated flow of new and exciting things coming unless there is constant new content. But if you have friends who like it? Or your neighbours watch it, or someone else at the book group, coffee morning, social club of choice in the 1960s, the more you are going to be able engage with it.

Official fan clubs and societies were no longer the only way to be fans together, it was much easier to find people and make your own purely due to the level of popularity of *Star Trek*, and across the pond, *Doctor Who*. The good Doctor did take a little bit longer to get the same level of fannish behaviour as *Star Trek*, despite starting three years earlier, but once it got going the fandom was just as strong and committed, with continuous high viewing figures well into the '90s, a popular magazine, fan letters, fan meets and conventions all starting up around this TARDIS-travelling timelord.

Within both of these fandoms you can see that the fans themselves, despite there being 120-odd years of content under the belts of both of them combined, have not changed. When William Hartnell stepped down as the Doctor in 1966 to be replaced with Patrick Troughton, a letter was written by a fan was rather unimpressed by this change: 'What have you done to BBC1's *Doctor Who*? Of all the stupid nonsense! Why turn a wonderful series into what looked like Coco the Clown?' wrote Mrs Estelle Hawken of Wadebridge, Cornwall, in a fan letter that now haunts the halls of *Doctor Who* fandom infamy. 'I think you will find thousands of children will not be watching *Dr Who* which up to now have been the tops.'

Pretty sure we could see that sort of comment on the *Doctor Who* social media boards every time the show changes anything. Fans, they never change.

It's around this time that the image of the fangirl and fanboy gets cemented into the public consciousness. Newsreels and magazines full of detailed reports of fans waiting for the favourite musicians, film actors and heart-throbs, depicted hysterical teens throwing themselves at their favourites. Beatlemania is characterised by the screaming girls and fans desperate for autographs alongside the Beatles–Rolling Stones rivalry in the fanbases. The BritPop battles of the '90s or the feud between Nicki Minaj and Cardi B are the same story told again. Pretty sure you would have found Regency fangirls doing the same thing with romantic poets or Jane Austen heroes. Darcy or Knightly? A question for the ages.

On the flipside to this, teenage boys reading comics, or getting involved in early gaming movements were seen as sad and lonely, hanging out in basements or going down the arcade to play endless games of pinball or *Pacman*. Either way you look at it, being a fan at this time was not cool, whoever you were, and there was an air of looking down on them that continued well up the age of geek-chic in the late '00s and 2010s. But it's definitely a good thing that fans of all ages stuck to their guns and kept on keeping on with what they loved.

Much like Holmes though, the bastion of pop culture that is *Star Trek* was nearly lost to us forever when the network decided to cancel it after one series. It was only due to the efforts of a dedicated network, letter writing, calling the studios and making themselves known as fans that changed the minds of the executives and kept the show from being pulled and making the world a lot lesser for it.

Star Trek has become synonymous with fan culture, and you'd be hard pressed to find anyone ready to 'engage' with the show or get 'beamed up' to watch at the dinner table.

Fans Work

'Zines, which had been a big part of fandom since the beginning, became very popular amongst *Trek* fans (Trekkers? Trekkies? Please let me know which one you prefer) and beyond as a way of communicating their ideas with each other. They had letters pages, art was included, discussion essays, even the stars of the show got involved. But what they also had was fanfiction, in the style of the type we would know today. The real deal, and they had, in some special 'zines, slash fiction.

If you don't know what slash fiction is, its is the umbrella term for fanfic about characters who are men being shipped together, with femslash being the equivalent for women. It gained its name from the forward slash symbol that was used between the characters names to indicate to the reader that this was a romantic relationship rather than a friendship. So if you saw Kirk/Spock you knew you were looking at shipping fanfiction.

What is notable about this is that Kirk and Spock are widely considered to be the first actively shipped same sex pairing. Fanfiction in the style of the show, getting the characters to act out new adventures or to be part of the crew yourself was very much a part of *Star Trek* fan culture, and spread out into other fandoms, but *Trek* fans were picking up on something that possibly no one really knew they were putting down, that Captain Kirk and the ever-logical Mr Spock might have a bit of a thing for each other. Now, who would have seen that coming? It's not like one of them flew into a primeval fury due to sexual lust and the two fought to the death in order to cure him of it with shirts being ripped open or anything. Thank you Pon-Far, the world of fandom would not be the same without you.

It isn't hyperbole to say that this ship changed the direction of fandom, as did many of the other ships to come out of *Star Trek*; remember the first interracial kiss on American television was between Kirk and Uhura. The show opened up the floor to so many ideas of what relationships could look like, either on purpose or, seemingly, by accident, including polyamory with Kirk, Spock and Bones frequently shipped as a trouple. The show that had always aimed to be progressive was making waves in the fandom the creators and cast couldn't have imagined, opening the way for a lot of people to look at the world differently.

Bearing in mind that gay relationships were still illegal in all of the countries that *Star Trek* was being shown in, writing this fiction, drawing art, or even discussing it was a taboo and so fans found ways of talking in code to figure out if it was safe or not to be talking about. A simple K/S was enough, but the major term used was "The Premise, allowing for many people, often women, to talk about ideas of sexuality and notions of change in a way that they hadn't before both through the 'zines and fanworks they created and in person. TrekCon, will you please make yourself known.

Get Your Con On

If you hit up a convention in the mid to late '60s you probably wouldn't recognise it as being anything like the conventions we have today. While cosplay, called hero costuming, future fashion or masquerade at the time, was present it was yet to be a major feature of the convention hall floor, mostly kept for the competitions during the event or a specialised party. You'd always be hard pressed to see the big media giants of cinema or TV advertising at events beyond showing up to do a panel. Mostly conventions were more for fans to meet, chat, discuss ideas on and off the panel stages and have a good time socialising. The core messaging is still there but there's no blow up, giant Pikachu in the main concourse.

Also, many events were pretty one track. You'd go to a sci-fi event for sci-fi, or a film event for film; the streams weren't in the habit of crossing, but a few things were about to see conventions bust through the comic book pages and out into the world of media legend. San Diego Comic Con would not have happened if it weren't for the *Star Trek* conventions that came before. Well, maybe it would, but a lot of what it is now and what it built into its nature as an event wouldn't have been there if it weren't for the *Star Trek* conventions. Nor would maybe others of the big events today. And you know why? Because Trek Cons pushed cosplay, costume making and competitions in a way that no one had done before.

It was the *Trek* events that started really including floor costumes as part of just being there. A Starfleet uniform is easy to make and wear on a con floor without it causing hassle for other con goers, something that was a definite no-no at many events. While this isn't to say that this wasn't happening at other conventions, it was more noticeably a theme at *Star Trek* cons. There is nothing quite like seeing a row of Spocks all lined up waiting to be called up to be judged or walking around the convention, looking at stands together.

The other big change that *Trek* cons had was the introduction of catwalk shows where costume makers and designers could strut their stuff without it being a competition or needing a skit or performance to be involved. It was purely about the look, focusing on sci-fi style fashion and bringing *Star Trek*'s alien characters to life. These shows were a big draw and conventions all over the world started replicating the walk-on style catwalk and masquerade for their competitions, making it a main stay of most conventions to this day, with San Diego Comic Con and others having their own dedicated fashion shows as part of the event.

Talking of SDCC. What San Diego brought to the party was that everyone was invited. Big movies were advertised as part of the event, including *Star Wars*, and shown alongside the stands for big name comic book creators or sci-fi lit authors. TV show panels happened for all different shows and the convention hall was packed with fans from all different parts of the fan-o-sphere. This was where comic con as we know it today was born.

Originally organised by a group of teenage comics fans from a basement in the city of San Diego, San Diego Comic Con was something of a pipe dream. They had one contact into the industry, a substantial amount of grit and hell of a lot of self-confidence.

They were sick of not being taken seriously, even amongst their fellow fans, with comics being seen as something for kids, and so decided to take matters into their own hands. They formed a committee and decided to visit the legendary comics artist, Jack Kirby, to ask for advice. Like I said, grit and self-confidence. That being said, the group were shocked when Kirby actually spoke to them and encouraged what they were doing with the words 'Do all of it', as one member, Mike Towry, recalled in a 2019 interview. So they did all of it.

The first three-day event was held in 1970, with two headline guests and tables of comics, art and books, and 300 people showed up. The next year it grew. And the next. And the next. With them opening up the floor to as many different types of media and fandom as they could, it became one of the biggest comic cons in the world.

San Diego Comic Con is now world renowned, with studios like Disney and Warner Bros using it as spring board to announce new projects and reach their fans and halls of artists and creators of all kinds interacting with the bustling corridors of fans who throng through the con. It's like nothing you've ever seen; even if you've been there, it's hard to believe it's real.

The work of fans like these, creating conventions, running 'zines, organising letter writing campaigns, are what truly shaped modern fandom. They built up the nature of what being a fan was, gave it structure and rules that pretty much everyone breaks because they are more like guidelines anyway, and showed the next generation a way to make their own spaces that would grow out of what was already there.

Into the Unknown

So, we all know what happens now right? The internet comes along and being a geek is suddenly super cool and everyone loves sharing their opinions about media with no fighting or arguing whatsoever and everyone lives happily every after... right? Right?

Oh. Maybe not. Well, that's a shame.

The world of fandom that had been spreading its roots for decades, building strong foundations that had already begun to grow into the strong communities around events like World Con and large fandoms like *Star Trek* and The Tolkien Society, had new blood coming in with the likes of *Star Wars*, *The X-Files* and a myriad of cult sci-fi and fantasy films with younger audiences who were ready to get involved.

Fan culture was ready for something new, it needed a new place to flourish, and the creation of an international space that could draw new people in and established fans together really did have a draw. What could go wrong with a new medium for people to share ideas on? Or post their fanworks for others to see and comment about?

Leonard Nimoy and William Shatner as Kirk and Spock in *Star Trek*, 1968.

Kirk and Spock off on an adventure.

A collection of fanzines from the 1970s, image by *stillunusual* on Flickr.

Kirk/Spock 'zine *Matter/Antimatter 1* cover by Mitchell Augustus Walker.

K/S and K.S. (Kindred Spirits): The APA
no. 9

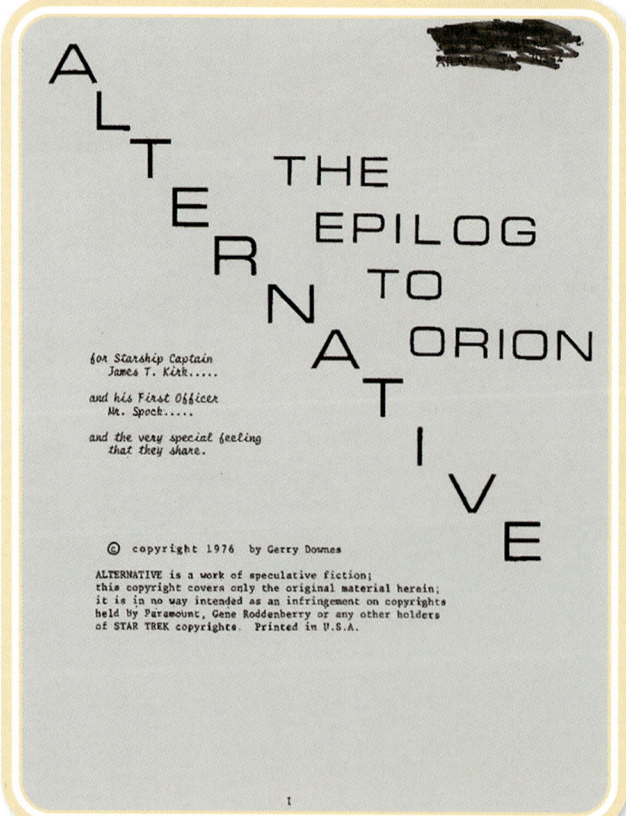

THE

ALTERNATIVE

EPILOG

TO

ORION

for Starship Captain
James T. Kirk.....

and his First Officer
Mr. Spock.....

and the very special feeling
that they share.

© copyright 1976 by Gerry Downes

ALTERNATIVE is a work of speculative fiction;
this copyright covers only the original material herein;
it is in no way intended as an infringement on copyrights
held by Paramount, Gene Roddenberry or any other holders
of STAR TREK copyrights. Printed in U.S.A.

Above left: Kindred Spirits
issue 9 scan from Bowling
Green State University.

Above right: Cover of
*Alternative The Epilog to
Orion* by Gerry Downes.

*Left: Alternative The Epilog to
Orion* title page by Gerry
Downen.

Let's Get Connected

'There were two of us [with the same first name] on the internet total in the 90s.'

There is something that seems a little ironic finding someone to talk to about what it was like to be part of old school online fandom on a new social media site. Or there would be if that site were not Tumblr, the still beating, if only just, heart of much of today's online fandom. Stumbling upon a graph discussing fans and fanfic in an incredibly academic way entirely by accident, I had to make time to talk with this Tumblr user full of knowledge and know-how on the inner workings of fandom: OlderThanNetfics (OTNF).

Author note: some of the people in this book preferred to be referred to by their usernames, or their real names are lost to fandom history somewhere in a dead forum, but the usernames are who they are in fandom. It also feels like a good reminder that fandom and fans have their own ways of working that include a level of anonymity that much of the internet appears to have lost.

An early adopter of online fandom spaces since her teens and, she has been through all the ups and downs of what being a fan means, especially one existing online. Talking with OTNF felt a little like being told the ancient magic by Aslan himself. She was there when it was written. Fact is, she wrote a lot of it.

> 'I got into the internet very young, like not for nowadays, but I got on technically when I was about eight or nine, which was at the end of the '80s. And I'm now 41. Gosh, wow. My stepfather was a big into technology, he was the head of networking at UC Berkeley at the time. So, he was like, "Oh, sh*t, a child. What do the children enjoy?" Well, what is entertaining in life? Well, what he thought was entertaining was hanging out on Usenet.'

And this is the moment I have to admit that I, despite being an long time, online fan myself, have no idea what Usenet is. How many of us do? I though AOL and Live Journal was the place this all started, but as with all fandom history, nothing is ever quite what it seems.

E-Newsletters and early Internet Spaces

Before the internet we know today there were closed networks, mostly provided by academic settings or tech companies. This was in the 1990s so many folks didn't even have a computer in their homes let alone be connected up to any sort of online network. So those who were spending any time online, and I'm sure no one will hold it against me to say this, were a little bit on the nerdier side of life. It will come as no surprise to know that these early users were therefore setting up spaces to connect with each other on the most important topics they could think of: fandom.

Don't worry, this isn't going to be a history of the internet because that's not what we're talking about, but it's useful to know a little bit about the setup of these primeval online spaces. Usenet in particular is the one that gets called up as the big starting point for online fandom, as well as mailing lists – more difficult to access and often needing certain know-how in the early days but increasingly becoming more open to everyone – and real time chat text-based spaces called Multi-User Dungeons (MUDs) were used for gaming, talking and more gaming.

Usenet predated the World Wide Web by a decade and was more of a conversational/chat tool accessed through a reader program like Outlook, for people to talk to each other; intended for keeping track of something more like a work discussion than if Muller and Scully were kissing, but it definitely got used for that.

Back to OTNF:

'It's almost like a mailing list. But it's more ephemeral. You could say it's like a forum, but I find in terms of platforms that I have used, I would probably liken Usenet more to an ephemeral mailing list than to use that at the time. It was very, like classic '90s internet, [old school].'

Unlike modern online spaces, or even the mailing lists of the time, Usenet posts and threads weren't saved and were deleted from servers within a few weeks, creating a certain type of fandom behaviour, such as posting links to 'slash' blogs or private websites, knowing that they would vanish soon enough without having to worry about them being tracked down later. You could also make comments or open up discussions that would then pretty much just disappear, something that could and was often taken advantage of for a myriad of reasons.

But they weren't all that different. We'd certainly recognise a level of cancel culture on these discussions and some of the earliest cultural battles in fandom were posed on Usenet, but there were still very closed spaces with their own ways of doing things and understanding of what fandom behaviour was. While they reached further than ever before, they weren't all that different from the fanclubs of the earlier part of the century. But of course, it was never going to stay like that.

When AOL brought in archiving news groups, opening up Usenet to more people outside of academia and tech, an influx of new users, newbies, came with them, and without even realising, challenged the existing small communities, if only by their sheer numbers, and it was almost impossible for these spaces to stay as they were.

The Kids are Alright

One of the big changes that came with this was online spaces suddenly allowing for more young people (teens) to become active members of the communities in a way that would have been almost impossible for many before, as they didn't have to leave their homes and could see what was happening outside of their own peer groups beyond the once-a-year trip to a convention, if they were lucky, or a local fan club if it existed.

A lot of pop culture is thought about as something of 'the youth', but in the case of organised fandom, for much of its existence before the internet it was developed and enjoyed by older people since they had the money and the access, and the time to engage with it properly. While much of what we think of as fan behaviour (I see you again, screaming fangirls) is centred around teenagers and the birth of the teenager as a concept, the nuts and bolts of fan culture and the practices that we still see today were created, for the most part by folks in their early twenties and older.

Young professionals and academics having time to go to clubs discussing science fiction and able to spend money on travel and magazines and the freedom of adulthood to do these things without having to ask for permission, housewives who would be able to buy themselves magazines and have the time to read them or write letters to other fans around the needs of their life, those working in and around universities or the tech industries having the need to use but also experiment with the internet and what it could do, these are obvious broad, sweeping strokes but they are all adults.

> 'What [my stepdad] probably was looking at were the many, many groups on there that were very industry-ish, because the only people who had access pretty much were people in the technology industry and people at universities.'

Being one of the few kids on the internet in the '80s and early '90s, OTNF remembers sticking out like a sore thumb when she first started getting active online. These weren't the multi-fandom, pop culture centric spaces that we picture forums of the '90s and '00s being, not by a long shot.

> 'You would have these news groups, that would be really high-level technical discussions that were maybe sort of snarky, but relatively well meaning and were sort of this kind of old-style discussion space. And I think the reason for that is, it's not that everybody was nicer. It's partly that there was no access and partly because the people who had access were 35-year-old white men who worked in [tech].'

This is not to say that fandom did not have a teen demographic pre-the internet but as we all know, when you're a kid, you do have to rely on the adults in your life for a lot of stuff. As child you would have to ask for money, permission, lifts, etc etc, ad infinitum. Add on top of that the possibility that the things we want to get involved in are not approved of by our parents/guardians – the Satanic Panic around DnD for example, see the final chapter for more on this – and it's not hard to see how teenagers and younger children would struggle to find a space in the fan sphere before the web becomes available to them.

You could definitely have your school club or meet ups with friends but for many being involved in fandom beyond those people you could cycle down the road to see, was out of reach. Being able to get online changed this, but it took time.

This is not to say that teens were not there and not involved but the level of presence that we see in online spaces today, and the focus on teen fans was not always what was there and still isn't. The internet changed, the fans didn't.

Enter the 1990s and 2000s.

Home computers were the big thing, and not just the big thing for tech professionals and the uber wealthy anymore but the big thing that people could afford and use without having to understand Linux inside out. Shiny white boxes with bouncing screensavers and user-friendly programmes, it was like the Starship *Enterprise* had come flying off the TV and dropped into the living room so you could dial up to the web from your landline – this makes me feel old. And there was always the local internet café if you didn't have a computer at home. Access to the web was now firmly in the hands of the wider public, and most importantly, the kids.

The Shape of Things To Come

'Bbbbbrrrwweeeqqquuukkkkkkk.'

One horrible noise later and a whole world of chatrooms, forums and email opened up to teenagers and they were going to make the most of it.

MySpace avatars of anime characters, music auto-playing on your chat profile, and being in with the comic creators on the *X-Men* boards were the coolest things you could have going for you in the '90s and '00s. People were starting to shape themselves new fandom lives online that they just didn't have access to at home. You couldn't go to school and talk with someone who was actually writing comic books and TV shows for a living, but you could if you got in on the right forum and stayed up until the USA came online.

People made their names online as a 'big name fan', all under usernames and anonymous icons that linked their online life to fan culture, but out in the rest of the world might just be 14-year-old with too much time on their hands. It didn't matter, fandom was going worldwide, and fans were excited to jump on this wild ride as early adopters and as some of the first online 'celebrities'.

However, the biggest change to fandom going online was being able to feel included without needing to open your mouth, or in this case, type out your thoughts. You didn't have to be in the physical fanclub and convention spaces anymore, you were involved simply by existing in the online fan-sphere. All it took was joining a forum, or making a LiveJournal account and you could start looking for what other fans were doing and seeing the discussions that were going on. You could lurk.

Now, that might not sound like a positive thing, but for a lot of folks, having the option to sit quietly in the corner and get the lay of the land instead of jumping in feet first is what made their fandom experience better, and these sites catered to that. Online spaces let you be as loud or as quiet as you wanted and provided you with every variety of forum, chatroom or blog in which to engage in the way that felt best to you. It gave people choice, and it helped people build the communities they wanted to build.

If one LiveJournal community was too rowdy for you, you could find some friends and go set up one that was more suited to you. If you wanted to share fanfiction but the others in one forum board weren't interested in that you went to find the one that was. Or you could float above the top of all of it dipping your toe in wherever you wanted to see what your fandom was doing in different places. It was legion of little, interlinked communities that all co-existed, often by not knowing that the others existed at all.

Fanworks continued to flourish online, as they had with previous up-ticks in technology. It wasn't uncommon for digital 'zines, or 'zines on disc to be made, and there were ones on floppy discs and made up as coded websites of their own, password protected for those who had access to look at. Fancams, clipreels of characters to music, started popping up, and sites actively dedicated to sharing and archiving fanfiction were getting more and more common. Fandom knew how to use the internet to its advantage.

But it wasn't to last.

With the rise of social media, this short lived 'golden era' of online fandom began to crumble. But, I hear you say, online fandom is huge, it hasn't disappeared or gone away so what's all this about it crumbling? And you would be right. In many ways, online fandom is doing more than it ever was. It's bigger, brighter, bolder, but has social media made it better? Or has it just made it different?

We should probably look into that.

WHY?

Finding Your Depth

It's May, and little chilly for the time of year but not so much that sitting outside is anything but pleasant, and considering that I have been sat outside for the last five hours discussing fandom in all its intricacies with Dr Vivian Asimos I am more than glad of that. Vivian is a public anthropologist, specialising in belief and fan culture. She is writing a book on cosplay which is part of the reason why we are sat here now enjoying a cup of tea and trying to pretend it is a balmier day than it is and making up for the fact that I was running late by getting to our second drinks.

We met at a convention a few weeks back and hit it off, in a very academic, nerdy way, both far too interested in each other's subject, me having been talking on cosplay at the event and also in the early days of planning this very book. What could be better than a chance meeting of minds?

'Think of fandom as a swimming pool,' she's saying, 'This is my party trick, but think of the swimming pool, that's how we should think of fandom.' I definitely haven't already slightly ripped off this analogy earlier in the book, but Vivian explains it better so, I'll let her explain.

> 'Perhaps it is better to think of belief [in this case fandom] as a community pool. There is a deep end, in which some may completely immersive themselves in the waters of belief, diving head-first into the waters. But there is an incline to the shallow end, where some may prefer to stand in the waist-height waters of belief. Others may wish to drift, paddling from one

end to the other, but never wanting to get their hair wet. And even others may want to simply sit on the side of the pool with only their feet in.'

Dr Vivian Asimos, "Everything is True Here, Even if it Isn't: the performance of belief online", *Journal of British Association for the Study of Religions*, 2020.

Sometimes the version described over coffee isn't quite as succinct as the version in the academic journal, but only sometimes.

It's so simple, so visually clear, such an easy way to explain to people, and golly don't I wish I had come up with it. It is something that I had been trying to put into words for years; how fandom can feel so different to different people and yet be the same thing.

Plenty of people would never use the word fan due to it having some of those connotations around the stereotypes of the hysterical fangirl or anti-social fanboy. Very few people identify themselves as either of those things even if they call themselves a fan so it would make sense that folks who are in the shallow end of the pool, or sipping the fruity, fan cocktail of media out on the sun loungers, don't see themselves as being part of this whole fandom malarky despite that being what they are. Vivian continues:

'Basically, belief is malleable, and people can play with the boundaries and elements of belief. Play here is important, it's serious but fun. Fans engage in a willingness to believe when first engaging with the piece of pop culture, and then can play with entering and exiting and blurring these bounds. That's when the pool metaphor can be used. So, a fan of *Lord of the Rings*, for example, can temporarily believe in the world when watching the movies, then believe in the core of what it's saying.'

We tend to associate the word belief with religion but, both belief and meaning are hugely personal things, unconnected with religion. They are how we define ourselves, how we place ourselves in society, how we learn who we are. We find our own depth and our own pool to swim in, the one that resonates with us best.

'These are various types of belief and living within the world and with others help to give shape to their worldview. Cause we use the stuff we have at our disposal to understand what the hell we're doing here on Earth.'

It comes back to that idea of finding a way to relate to the world around, looking at what you know and understand and seeing it reflected in the stories that you are told. We all do it. For some it has more meaning than others but we do find that meaning there in some way. Once it was using gods and goddesses throwing tantrums under the ground, or spirits weaving their tales in the heavens, to explain phenomenon we couldn't explain, now we're using them to delve into and understand different social issues or scientific ideas and we connect to the characters used to help through those ideas just as much as we did in the past.

These are our modern myths. These are core parts of our understanding of ourselves whether we recognise it in the open way of a fan or not. Myth infects all our lives, and we make meaning out of it in some way; media and fandom do that as much as any other cultural element, if not more so. We make them part of ourselves, and that will look different depending on what end of the pool we are in.

1 Modern Myth

'Fan Fiction is a way of culture repairing the damage done in a system where contemporary myths are owned by corporations instead of by the folk.'

Henry Jenkins (Director of Media Studies at MIT)

Fanfiction! Ah, got your attention there, but just wait a moment, we're not quite there yet. And yes, I know it's why a lot of you picked up this book, you naughty, naughty fic readers you, but this will cycle back to fanfiction properly, promise.

I know we keep talking about it and not exactly explaining what it is, but be patient my little adventurers, we'll get there, we'll get there. There's a reason I want to talk about meaning and finding yourself in fan spaces first.

There's a lot of understanding needed about why people become fans, it is something that a lot of society thinks of as a strange little hobby, outside of the obvious sports acceptation which definitely doesn't have deep roots into the misogyny of everyday life and how certain types of masculine-coded behaviours are seen as the norm, but that is getting away from the point when actually, sports fans are a perfect way to explain all other fans. Why wouldn't they be? They are fans after all.

Picture if you will, a football fan. They go to support their team, big or small, on a regular basis, they may be in the stadium every week with their life member, season ticket. They never miss a match. It's important to go. This fan is decked out in all the gear, the hat, the refillable cup, the favourite player's shirt, and they even have a homemade scarf. This fan is singing every chant, they know all the words, and they are feeling every up and down of the game. They come with friends and family, maybe they have been coming since they were a kid with their parents, and now they bring their kid; it's a thing that connects them to the people they love and the community around them. Now replace all that with *Stranger Things*.

Is it so much weirder that it's a Netflix show about a kid with superpowers that people are obsessed with rather than a sport? A lot of people don't get the intensity of either type of fan, but they are a lot less likely to give you a strange look if you say you're going to the football than if you say you're going to Comic Con. When you really get into it, football fan, media fan, boyband fan, it all has the same thing at its heart, a love for the story.

But football isn't a story? Right? Wrong.

The game has a narrative, it has characters, heroes and villains, it has epic highs and tragic lows, it pulls you along with the emotional thread that is akin to anything upon the Grecian stage or silver screen. And it's a long running story too: you know the history of your team, the players who have come and gone, the trophies they've brought home, all of it, in much the same way that guy in the hellfire club t-shirt knows the difference between a demigorgon, a mind flayer and Vecna without blinking an eye. Whether this knowledge comes directly from *Stranger Things* or having a good working knowledge of *Dungeons and Dragons* will vary from person to person, as there's a decent amount of crossover in that Venn diagram of nerdom.

In many ways it is the act of storytelling and of wanting to be part of that story that makes us fans. We want to show our passion, our love, how we connect to that story, and place ourselves in the folklore that is built up around them. Is it not so that the 1966 World Cup is a thing of legend? Or '86 and the literal hand of God that has become one of the defining moments of British sports lore that even the least of sports fans, let's say someone who possibly watched the Women's Euros and maybe some of those odd sports in the Winter Olympics, knows it as a part of our social consciousness in much the same way that you must have been living under a rock to not know that Darth Vader is Luke's father – and if you didn't I am not calling that a spoiler, come on, it's 2023.

Going back to the early parts of the first chapter, there is something very inherently human about enjoying stories, however we engage with them. They help us process thoughts, feelings, memories, emotions, and all those things that bounce around inside our brains and need to be hooked onto something that is just that little bit easier to comprehend than abstract blobs and colours masquerading as the central core of our beings.

We start trying to explain those ideas with characters who do the work for us, play it out in make believe in one way or another, and we don't just explain our own selves like this, we explain the whole world like this. What the hell is lightning? It's there because some anthropomorphic figure of human failings is cross – yeah, Zeus, I said what I said. Those pretty lights in the sky that move and go all sorts of colours at night? Spirits and magic, or possibly charged particles hitting the Earth's atmosphere, but even if you know that, you can't help but believe the folklore when you see the Northern Lights.

My goodness this feels pretentious but there we are, can't get into the philosophy of all this without a little bit of waffle about human nature now, can we? All pretentiousness aside, we find meaning in stories of all kinds, and the way that they can connect us with others. We could be sat around the fire in a great Viking hall listening to the great stories of gods and mischief, or we could be in the cinema watching stories of gods and mischief. The myths of our modern age are the ones that we are shown through our media, you can track back many of the heroes of our age to those who came before – the most literal and obvious being Thor and Loki in the Marvel comics and films, but Superman is a retelling of Moses, and how many times have people retold the Arthurian legends through different lenses?

It's all much the same really, you can have a story open with 'once upon a time' or 'a long time ago in a galaxy far, far away' and there is all the different of a change of location really, expect one thing. These modern myths, they are fixed. They have canon that cannot be changed, they exist as a fixed thing, a film, a book, a piece of media with copyright and trademarks owned by someone or some corporation more likely, which brings us back to the quote I opened this chapter with from Henry Jenkins:

> 'Fan Fiction is a way of culture repairing the damage done in a system where contemporary myths are owned by corporations instead of by the folk.'

If we see the stories of our modern age as folklore, then why are we only shown one point of view? A tightly held, controlled point of view? It narrows down life experience to only a select group of people with everyone having to relate themselves to those people and ideals as best they can. Thing is, that's really hard to do, particularly when the people who are like you become the puppets that are acting out prescribed roles around the main character's story. We all know the stereotypes of the killed-off girlfriend, or the comedic black best friend, the angry mother-in-law, or the scarred villain. There are any number of cookie cutter caricatures that come out of the Hollywood movie machine. It affects us and send those who are not represented as the hero of the piece looking for stories elsewhere.

Except those stories, until recently, have been few and far between. That's where fanfiction, fanart and fandom comes in.

Fanworks like folk lore, are a way to start changing of the text through the lens of personal experience and show why it's important that we look to these 'great works' and change them to fit our own narratives. You suddenly see who is missing from the story when you see the tags like 'genderbent' or 'trans!AU' for example on a fanfic, or a piece of fanart depicting a western, white character as another race or cultural background. People are putting themselves and their world view into a story that has been a tightly held-in version of society up until that point.

It's the same thing that bards and storytellers of the past would have done. You change the story to the reflect the people you're telling it to or the space you're telling it in both literally and figuratively.

There is a reason why so much of fandom is full of those who don't quite fit in with the societal norms, who prefer fantasy to football, or who are looking for escapism, because much of fandom allows for a level of revisionism. If you don't see yourself in the world, in the media or the folklore, you find your own hall, one that is fit for the person you are, and you retell it for yourself and those who want to listen.

Above, opposite and overleaf: No matter who you are. (Photography by Megaera Amis)

Above and below: Fandom comes in all shapes and sizes.

Above and opposite: Mage Knight Board Game by Farley Santos, Creative Commons BY-SA 2.0.

2 A Touch of Familiarity

When I was a kid, my parents used to read to me. That's what lots of parents do; it was and is a special moment with parent and child that not only starts the educational thing of reading, but also creates moments of familial connection between you. I am dyslexic, and it took me a long time to learn to read, but I loved stories – always have done, and still do – so my parents making time to read to and with me meant a lot. One of my earliest memories of this, while I was still struggling, is my dad reading me *The Hobbit*.

Okay, so why are we going down this strange little memory lane? Because I now, as an adult human, have tattoos from *The Hobbit* and *The Lord of the Rings* on my body. I have all the extended editions of the films, I have art books, statues, Warhammer figures, cosplays, replica props, I have made friendships due to it, I cry when I hear the opening bars of *Concerning Hobbits* play. It is the fandom that I hold the closest to my heart and it is my oldest fandom. It's the first thing I would have said I was a fan of. That's because of my dad.

He didn't know he was doing that. He was simply introducing me to something that he loved and wanted to share with me. It was important to him that I had enjoyed it. He may later have regretted it considering for quite how many years it became my everything, but he went out of his way, both my parents did, to encourage my enjoyment of it as a child and for a good chunk of time afterwards. It became something that we did together, and was our connection point to each other in ways that I can't even explain. The fandom that will always mean the most to me is the one that I shared with my dad.

And I am not the only one.

I said in the introduction that fandoms come and go, that some are long running loves and others are flashes that vanish as quickly as they came, and I think its right to think about them as loves, because as with romances that we have in our lives, no matter how trivial, they leave a mark on us in some way. They are part of who we are going forward. Perhaps the love of a lifetime, or a high school sweetheart that never quite panned out how you hoped, or that one night stand that comes up in an embarrassing way when your friends want to tease you, or maybe the one that broke your heart and you can't think about without that crushing weight of emotion hitting you in the stomach – anytime I think about Obi-Wan or Ahsoka confronting Vader, it's tragic and I can't not feel that no matter how ridiculous *Star Wars* can get.

This emotional connection is a large part of why that is. Yes, we all find things on our own, stumble across something that cannot help but make our brain go 'brrrrr' from time to time, but for a large number of us that first point of contact is through a family member, a close friend or a partner, even into later life. You take an interest because someone you love is sharing something with you, and you want to share that with them.

There are plenty of people who don't like football, but it's important to them to do it with their parents or partner because the people they care about love it. There's no shortage of people who'll go down the pub on a Saturday to talk the footy for some one-on-one time with that emotionally distant family member because that's the way that they can share in something together.

There's a closeness, and intimacy in it, a bond. Whether you are actually interested at the end of the day or not, and when this emotional connection happens as a child it often becomes a core part of who we are, hardcore fandom not pertaining.

Professor Paul Booth is a professor of Media and Cinema Studies at DePaul College of Communication in Chicago – I told you we'd come back to Paul. Everyone say 'hello' – and a long-time fan of *Doctor Who*. He's written a huge amount about fandom, and has a large amount of *Doctor Who* and *Star Trek* merch behind his head from what I can see in the Zoom window. It's these moments when you know you're with your people.

Much like myself, Paul considers his fandom to be part of who he is. It's a part of his identity, stemming out of the childhood memories and familial moments that drew him to it in the first place.

'My dad watched [*Doctor Who*] and introduced it to me, my family is British. He watched the first episode in 1963, a behind the sofa type thing. And so, when I was growing up, we would watch it together, and then I started watching it on my own. There's a very strong emotional childhood connection to it. It makes me feel like a kid again when I watch it.'

The emotional connection of childhood is a powerful one, but also a very simple one. The emotions you have around something from your childhood, are to a greater or lesser extent going to remain those of a child, and it's hard for that not to be the case. That's how you experienced it, with no lens of adulthood or any complexities that might occur to you in later life. It's an emotional rose-tinting of the subject. It's why something in your memory of it will never be as big, or dramatic, or exciting once you've grown up, and that is the same with media.

Have you ever had that moment of sharing something you loved as a kid with a friend who's never seen it, and they just can't get it? This is why. You have memories of it that may well not be anything to do with what the content of the media is, but make it part of who you are. Your friend just doesn't have that and so isn't getting the same nostalgic, emotional payoff that you are getting.

What it does mean is those connections we have to the media of our childhood, particularly ones that grew into fandoms, *Doctor Who* for Paul and *The Lord of the Rings* for me, also stay like that. These are fandoms that run deep, like a seam of mithril through us, that maybe don't even surface very often but always feel like going home, because that's what they are. Comfort. Home. Love. Identity. The building blocks of ourselves as people in whatever way that might be.

'I'm obviously a *Doctor Who* fan, I've got a lot of stuff. It's part of how I identify myself, right? This is where I teach my classes from, this is where I do the Zoom meetings from. I'm not disguising that. In fact, it's somewhat deliberate. So that if someone else is a *Doctor Who* fan, they could be like, "Oh, let's talk about *Doctor Who*" or whatever. I've made it a part of my identity. I've made it a part of who I am. It's not everything I am. But it is a significant part. And it's an obvious part, it's a part that I'm performing that I want people to know about me.

Let's then say that we're having this interview and you're like "Wow, *Doctor Who* was like the worst show I've ever seen, and I really hate every single part of it. Anyone who likes *Doctor Who* is you know, should be locked up." That's not just insulting *Doctor Who*, because you see that *Doctor Who* is important to me. I think it's like that, with lots of as fandom, has become more visible, and as it's become more a part of people's lives in a public way it becomes maybe, not more attached to it but more or less reflective of who you are. It's how you want to be identified. And so, an insult or someone not liking it becomes more personal.'

But this isn't the only story I heard about this sort of thing. Almost without fail, every single person I spoke to had a picture-perfect memory they could pinpoint, when someone important in their life invited them in to enjoy something together. No matter what age they were, those formative points that brought them to loving something in a way that they knew was beyond just 'Oh, yeah, that's cool'.

Fandom is personal, each of us has our own personal identity grown around how we digest the stories that come into our lives, but how they enter our lives is just as important in that blossoming identity. Fandom is personal, sure, but fandom is also connection and community, and having those as part of our fannish journey makes our experience and our own self expression as a fan something more, and hopefully something better.

3 Welcome to the Tribe

It's probably time I, the guide that you have all entrusted yourselves to, fessed up to something. *Stands, clears throat* I… am a fan. A big one. I love being a fan. Can't get enough of it. What do you mean you already knew? Well, okay, sure, can't get too mad about you figuring that one out now, can I? It's not like my house is full of fanart, cosplay and all the signs that I might well like some very nerdy things. Or that I have tattoos of my fandom favs permanent inked into my skin. Nah, couldn't be me. Expect…

I have made fandom part of my being, literally. It's something that I see as a formative part of who I am, and it would be fair to describe me as a body puppeteered by all of the personality traits of all the characters I've ever loved, and some that maybe called me out as a person a little too much, and I'm okay with that. But that wasn't always the case.

Show of hands, how many of us have felt a little different? Maybe your interests were a little too passionate, or you didn't like the same thing as your peers. You felt isolated until you stumbled across folks like you, the ones who your certain brand of fannish behaviour made sense to. Or maybe you're the other side of that coin, one of the fans whose 'thing' was in the mainstream. After all, fan culture is basically a horseshoe of intensity. How far into the thing did you get before you were dressing up in silly outfits and screaming about how much you love it from the bleachers, huh? I see you Barmy Army, you can't hide in the sports corner, get out here and be counted with the rest of us fandom nerds. For those that don't know, this is a sub-set of England cricket fans who show up to matches in elaborate outfits and like to let their support be known in some pretty over-the-top ways.

Either way, what made you the fan you are was the people who were there enjoying the thing with you. And it's also true that whatever way you come into fandom, if you're a little bit too on the OTT side of things, other people struggle to quite understand it, but once you have your tribe, it doesn't matter that much anymore.

At some point all of us find our tribe, no matter how strange their rituals and traditions might be, we all know it when we see it, these are our people. It's why community builders, those who set up the fanclubs, or the forums, who moderate them, or encourage people to join, are so important. My own first, personal, experience of this was a local librarian – ook! – and my goodness what would we do without librarians. She started an anime club for kids and saw an awkward pre-teen checking out *Fullmetal Alchemist* manga every weekend and opened the door for me to find a new group of people. I don't think I'd be writing this book without her, and she was not the first, nor the last fan community builder who has changed mine, and other people's lives for the better, including their own.

Roger, Roger, Captain Rex

It is a few months into the research for this book and a campaign is making its way around *Star Wars* Twitter. It's a campaign to get a fan into one of the new shows, or in some way to be part of the franchise. It's not new for big name fans to be included in some way in marketing or as creators in franchises like *Star Wars* but this one felt different. It was calling out to me. I had to talk to this person.

Michael Cannavo, aka Rexin Around, is the ultimate *Star Wars* fanboy, and I mean that in the best and most positive way. He is a community builder, and has supported and pushed for much-needed change within a fandom that is more than a little infamous for how it treats creators, actors and other fans alike. If you don't remember how bad the backlash against the Prequel Trilogy was, then you are lucky. But there are fans, like Michael, who have made it their business to not only change the community and behaviours that already exist but to develop spaces that shape new and improved approaches to being a fan.

'I think we all kind of followed this trajectory a bit where we were fans when we were younger, got into high school age, and I kind of suppressed it a bit.' Michael is sat in his home office on Zoom with me. The whole background is full of clone trooper helmets on display – as a fellow *Star Wars* fan, it's hard not be jealous of his extensive collection – and we've already geeked out about it a little. How could we not? It's a point of connection between us, instant common ground.

'I was always wearing *Star Wars* shirts or talking about *Star Wars* or drawing pictures of Darth Vader on my tests. But it was never like, my identity in high school. And I felt really lost. Like, I didn't have a best friend in high school; I knew everybody, but I had no one to talk to. And, and as a result, after high school, I just found myself completely alone. Like depressingly, by myself. Everybody went off to university and I didn't, I wasn't able to afford it. And it was a disaster. I went to community college, and I tried really hard, but I was severely depressed. I look back, and I don't even recognise that version of myself. Then one day, I started just driving around to different stores just to be like, I'll go walk around and see people, just try to be out in public. So, I put my headphones in, and walked into this discount store here. They had all these action figures for like three bucks apiece, and they were *Star Wars* action figures. I was like "Oh my gosh, like these have gotten so good over the last few years", because I hadn't collected since I was a kid. And I bought them all.'

It's hard not to relate to this in some way as we talk. I've been there, and I'm sure that many, if not most fans, have at some point. There is definitely a feeling of being in that place, lost and unsure of yourself since the standard social aspects of life don't fit you that well. For Michael this was a moment of, not quite inspiration, but of the beginning of change, collecting figures, driving for miles to find different stores and spending hours hunting for every type of *Star Wars* toy, action figure and statue he could find.

'I would like chart a map and say like, okay, these are the fifteen stores I'm going to hit up in San Diego County or LA County. It just became like an obsession. It became a hobby, and I felt very fulfilled doing it. But I also felt alone. So, I made a YouTube video. And I titled it *Star Wars fan looking for a community*. Looking back, it's so funny because it's just like it's it was really cringy and also a little bit desperate. But it worked.'

Michael is grinning and shaking his head as he's talking, pinpointing the actions that brought him into the *Star Wars* fold.

'I remember being like, "Oh my gosh, like, this is it. This is where I find friends." I joined the Facebook groups for collectors. It was the early days of like, any sort of community and online because it was like Facebook had just started. I met so many people that were like, so generous, and we would trade the figures with each other.

They would surprise me with stuff, I'd surprise them; it was like this unbelievable community. This kind of got me started in thinking, I love community, this is what I want to do. I'm a community builder.'

Michael is not the only person with a story like this. There are as many of these stories as there are fan communities, or more, because those communities simply would not exist if these moments didn't happen. Because not every fan is a community builder themselves, but they still need a community to go to, or we are all lost in an ocean that doesn't quite get us with no sign of land. Or worse, land that is only hospitable if we change ourselves in someway to fit it.

The unofficial-ness of this type of community, the one you might run across through YouTube videos, or on a Twitter thread, is what really makes it work for newcomers, or those looking for a new way to be a fan, in a way that perhaps the old school official clubs and groups do not. This is an easy space to float, to watch, to see if you fit without making a commitment. You don't even have to have an account for the sites in many cases, so you can just take your time whilst still feeling involved, which is what a lot of people, scarred from years of social difficulties, need. We all have a few old wounds in one way or another.

Community builders, like Michael, have not only invited people to the table, but they are also letting you in without needing to be invited in the first place.

'I started my YouTube, and videos were blowing up, they were getting hundreds of thousands of views, every single one. And I didn't really understand why. And so, I just kept doing what I was doing, showing the behind the scenes of how to build armour, and being in the 501st, it was all very club related.'

For those who don't know, the 501st is a *Star Wars* costuming group that is regarded in some ways as the official costuming group of the franchise. There's a lot of kudos to being part of it but also a lot of rules around creating and wearing costumes in order to uphold the standards of the club. It's not for everyone but for some it's how they want to get involved in fandom.

'When we would go to events, I would flog [the armour], and it made me very loved and hated because the older people in the clubs were like "stop showing people how we do this", and the younger people in the clubs are like "I'm here because of you". I became very divisive in a way because of just the different angle I took. I think a lot of people then kind of became very fake and I was aware people were latching on to me for the wrong reasons. It was such a weird sort of petty dynamic, and I started to learn like this is fake, like, this is all fake, and this is hurting a lot of people.

I remember there was one cosplayer who was an older guy, and he had a son. I think about him a lot, because he was so clearly a fan of what I was doing. But he wore like a Party City Captain Rex suit. [Party City is a US Halloween costume brand.]

And he would always be like "Hey, look at us, like fellow Rexes" and I was never rude to him, but I never gave him the time of day. And that sits with me a lot that it was like, because this guy was so nice. And I'm so bummed that I missed out on a friendship with him that because he's gone. He probably just got tired of the community, understandably, and I and I look back and I was like, I'll never let that happen again, I will never miss out on getting to know a beautiful human being because his costume didn't look like mine.'

The thing that community builders do, isn't just bringing a space to life, but it's actively being the people that they needed when they were the one struggling and seeing the mistakes that they have made in the past when they could have been that person for someone. It's looking at yourself, learning from where you messed up and putting the best of what you and your fandom could be out into the world for others.

This is opposite of gatekeeping, it's opening Dr Vivian Asimos's swimming pool on the first day of summer and letting everyone enjoy it as they please. There is no right way to be in these spaces, as long as *everyone* is, in fact, enjoying themselves. That is something that Michael wants to make sure that he is always checking in himself and the fans who have joined him in his community.

'I talked about this openly a lot because it was a sort of like a coming to the light moment. I wanted people around me to know about it because I had set an example for so many people. I wanted them to know, like, I don't feel this way. I don't feel this way anymore. It's ridiculous and childish. I became very opposite of what everything the club was, encouraging people who were home building their costumes, encouraging silly, goofy videos, in movie accurate suits, like, let's have fun and enjoy the space. And I kind of got everything completely shifted, and it was, is, for the better.'

People like Michael are a big part of why fan culture is now bigger than ever before, not simply because the more people can connect, the more they open themselves up to new ways of thinking and wanting to be part of a bigger, better community, but these spaces also show why they are connecting and what they are doing with that connection. The world is getting weirder because are seeing that they aren't alone, and they can be their happy, weird selves in spaces that are built and grow because of that weirdness.

You can join fanclub after fanclub and find that none of them fit you, but then one day you stumble on a Discord server or a Twitch community that feels like a second family the moment you enter the chat. Or it may be that you spend a long time being the big name in a fandom only to decide to retire from public fan life just to hang out with your friends in a boardgame café and hit up Comic Con once a year. You're allowed to ebb and flow and find new or different ways to interact with the things that bring you joy, because that's the most important thing, that you are still getting joy from them. The moment that they no longer spark it, Marie Kondo that stuff and embrace the things that do.

But it's hard to find your people if you don't know where to look for them. Sometimes they are an ocean away just waiting for you to show up. It's a good thing that there are those out there sending out a flare to be the guide they needed when they were lost at sea.

Part of the Whole

We could walk over 500 different journeys into fandom and 500 more again looking at all the ways that people find themselves in this strange little corner of society, and each of them would likely come back to the point of connection. The meaning we find in stories links us to the people around us, to new people who move into the spheres we share, to people thousands of miles away who we might never meet but we share a common point of love and enjoyment.

In 2022 I was at Dublin Comic Con, working as a judge and panellist for the cosplay competition. One of my fellow judges was a woman, around my age, who hadn't been able to bring her costumes with her. Instead, she was laying out pictures of them on a table, beautiful images of costumes and locations that I didn't recognise. It quickly became clear that these images were not all of her, nor were they all by one photographer or one group of cosplayers. It was a spectrum of fandoms, crafts and people that she was covering every inch of the table with. They were all cosplayers from Ukraine, and she was a refugee.

She hadn't been able to bring any costumes to the convention, not because she couldn't get them on a plane, an issue that I had been having, but because she hadn't had time to do more than grab a bag and flee her home. We talked about being a cosplayer for a long time, about her builds, the people she'd worked with, the costumes she'd planned for the future, all the things any cosplayer would talk about, all the while placing images of cosplayers from all over Ukraine on the table. We talked about their stories too, she had them all written down to share with us.

It's hard not to tell a story like this and not feel like you are attempting to pull on heartstrings. And maybe I am a little, but being able to find that point of connection, the same meaning that we both had in who we were as people, was, and is, a very important thing. When we see our own interests and identity, because that is what fandom is, reflected in someone we are able to see them as more than just another NPC outside of our bubble of existence.

There are plenty of moments in all our lives that are like this, especially when major things like wars are so hard for us to relate to when they aren't affecting us directly. Now, I'm not going to say that fandom is going to save the world, it's clearly not, but anything that may well allow us to cut through everything else and see someone else as familiar or open the door to learning about life experiences other than our own must have some worth.

We were in the same swimming pool and we didn't even know it, but the second we did, we could jump in the deep end and share in it together for the briefest of moments.

Why do we do fandom? Because it adds to our self-knowledge and the knowledge of this ridiculous place that we exist in. We see something in it that we relate to or that compels us in some way. It connects us in every sense of the word. And possibly also throws a spanner in the works every so often when it overwhelms us, and we have to step away. It will always be there to have you back though, don't worry, just waiting to see what you'll do next.

Above: Fandom Fun at Rexin' Around.

Below: Michael on set of *Kenobi* with Ewan McGregor.

Above: Commander Cody and Captain Rex cosplays.

Left: Not shown, the writer squeeing over this Tech cosplay off screen.

Opposite: Michael and Grogu are the stars of the show.

It's all about community.

You know what, I think Michael might like *Star Wars*.

WHO? AND HOW?

Making it Fanwork

If there is one thing that always gets brought up about fandom, it's fanfiction. Couldn't tell you for why, but it does. Hard to miss it really. It seems to be the thing that anyone outside of fan spheres will bring up as 'oh that strange thing that fans do' and often it's a bit of a joke. It's brought up whenever folks talk about Comic Con or other big fan events, even when discussing online fan communities 'oh yeah, they are probably writing smutty fics about stuff'. We've all heard or read the comments. We see journalists bring it up in interviews with celebs: anyone remember the infamous moment in fandom history when Caitlin Moran put Benedict Cumberbatch and Martin Freeman on the spot with a slash fic reading on a *Sherlock* press event? Not exactly a shining moment for any fan.

And focusing on fic is hardly fair, since (a) it is for fans, by fans, within their own communities, (b) there is more to fanworks and fan-expression than fanfics, and (c) fanworks are, and always have been, an expression of boundless love and admiration.

Because that's what all of it is, its fans showing other fans they love the thing. And fiction is a popular way to do that. It is, in many ways, the quickest and easiest to engage in – I say with my third cup of tea of the morning as I struggle on through writing this introduction – as it requires little set up beyond the ability to put words on a page, unlike say fanart or fancams that may well need more equipment or money in one way or another. You can do it anonymously on sites dedicated strictly to fanfiction, and it's really popular with other fans. All of these things give fanfiction the kudos of most people's first gateway into creating fanworks, with fanart coming a close second, and being the way that they find communities to expand their interest within.

But that's not all there is. Fanart flip-flops between being seen as a thing of beauty to being something a bit 'cringe' by those on the outside, and let's be honest, on the inside too, though I think we all know that we've all been a 13-year-old with a crush drawing side character number eight from our favourite anime/comic/film/video game/delete as appropriate at one time or another. There's nothing wrong with cringe. Cringe culture is dead, long live cringe.

But there is more to fanwork than this. People are constantly finding new ways to explore what is going on inside the heads of their favs, or challenge the narrative of the story. If you don't think a playlist about Sansa Stark's rise from trauma and destruction won't have you crying into the ground by the end, you're wrong.

Finding a way in and plugging into the maelstrom of thoughts and feelings that we often get after engaging with something that truly moves us in some way is an important part of processing. A story trying to tell us something is no good if we can't work through all the elements that electrified us in a way that cements the emotional message. For some people that's talking about how good a movie was and for others it's going home and drawing hundreds of pictures of blorbos one and two holding hands – or... *something else*.

Is it a bit silly? Yes. Is it a great cultural work? Maybe not. Does that make it something we shouldn't do? Absolutely not.

The tendency to put it into a box of 'unimportant' creations as compared to 'proper' works of art, fiction and criticism by those in and out of fandom alike is dismissive of both the works themselves and their creators simply because they are the words and inner workings of ordinary, everyday people expressing themselves in a way that they deem fun for no monetary or social value other than their own enjoyment. Honestly, if a historian stumbled upon a pile of fanart from a peasant in sixteenth century England depicting their favourite biblical characters or the local lords hanging out with them, they'd be punching the air.

Okay, I did promise. I'm not doing pull reveal into another topic this time, we really are going to talk about fanworks now: why people do them, how they go about creating them and putting them out into the world and all the various things that come with that. It's the good stuff, right? It's how fans interact with each other, with the creators they admire (both media creators and other fan creators), with the work itself and as a way to express those things we were talking about in the last chapter.

This is where you tell your stories. Make the myth your own however you choose to do it.

1 Affirmative and Transformative

When it comes to engaging with fandom, it's all different strokes for different folks. Trying to quantify the ways that people get involved in their fandom, and who those people are, is actually quite tricky. It's not simply fanfiction, collecting and meets and that's the extent of how people can be a fan. You can't, as much as we might want to, strictly classify everything into categories that define each fan as a certain type. I say that as we are about to try and build some categories to drop certain types of fanworks into.

So, okay. There is nuance, but we are going to ignore it to start with, just to get our heads around the basics. Then we can play around a little and make up our own minds about all this.

This little sub-chapter has been bouncing this around book since the beginning, because when you're talking about fandom, you have to, eventually, get into these definitional terms. Start drawing up boundary lines around things, what goes in what box, what counts as what, who gets to keep what type of thing in the big, weird fandom divorce that seems to have happened over the years, that possibly was never really a joined thing in the first place, or maybe it was. I've certainly seen arguments a hundred comment threads long that couldn't decide this, but what it all led to was somehow needing to include it here, in this book.

The Affirmative and the Transformative.

And golly have I gone over it more times than the people in those threads (well, maybe not) because I wasn't sure if I actually wanted to talk about it beyond the definitional points so that you would all know what it meant and we could move happily along talking about fic and myth and making community spaces etc, etc. But that's just not possible, is it? I said it myself, right at the top of the book, we can't just have a definition and move on. We could, but what sort of explorers would that make us? Hardly going into the wild depths of fandom if we just sit here and look at what folks have done before, especially since there are plenty of folks out there with ideas that we haven't met yet. Can't write that off.

The terms were coined in an essay by user obsession_inc in 2009 which was posted on Dreamwidth and cross-posted to LiveJournal: 'I'd like to propose my own definitions: affirmational fandom vs. transformational fandom.' – obsession_inc

She goes on to detail the differences she has noticed between these two, and how they may play out. It was then built on by user damned_colonial who solidified the definitions of what each grouping was.

Author note: I am honestly obsessed with the usernames of 90s and 00s fandom spaces. The only place you really see this sort of username over real name behaviour is on Tumblr for the most part and I am sad about that. There's something about calling someone only by a username that is so embedded in fandom culture, and I hope never leaves.

Now, it's highly doubtful that either of these users had any idea that these discussions of fandom meta, building on other users' ideas and discussions as they were, would become something that would be used in academic studies of fandom or as the major terminology that would come to dominate the conversation around fandom styles. And I certainly don't think that they believed it would be anything more than a way of categorising some of these fan activities. In fact, obsession_inc stated right at the beginning of her essay:

> 'Before doing so (and at the risk of becoming too twee to stand myself), let me just say that I see both sections as celebrational fandom, first and foremost, and that there is a lot of joy and effort and creativity put into both, and that there is a certain amount of crossover. These are just the majority trends, as I've seen them. [Apply giant grain of salt.]'
>
> *obsession_inc, Affirmational fandom vs*
> *Transformational fandom, 2009*

Which is of course true. But we humans do love to propose opposites, don't we? Cat or dog? Apples or oranges? Pink or blue? Which one? What camp do you fall into? I think we can all see that this might cause some... issues? Though no more than were there before, just now with added labels, which always goes down so well. But before we even go there, let's take a little bit of a deeper look into how Affirmative and Transformative have now been defined. Because... knowing is half the battle.

Affirmative – Collecting, Canon-compliant etc.

Let's start with that nice description from the top of the book:

> Affirmative Fandom is one of the two types of fandom that is defined within fan studies and fan spaces. Affirmative Fandom tends to refer to fans who: are creator-centric, and who collect, analyse, archive, and affirm the canon of media. An example of affirmative fandom could be The Tolkien Society, community events such as WorldCon or critical works on a topic of media.

This pretty much runs along the lines of our two fandom-defining LiveJournal and DreamWidth users.

What this means in a broader, definitional, categorising sort of way, is that Affirmative Fandom is the act, within fan spaces, of affirming the canon. That sounds very serious, but this affirmative method can come in all sorts of shapes and sizes: collecting books, action figures, memorabilia, etc; discussion of the media through meta essays, vlogs or conventions; attending panels or talks with the creators, cast and crew of the piece of media; it's basically only engaging with the 'canon' elements of the media in some way. This might mean that you are more likely to play new DLCs or video games rather than read or write a fanfic to get more content from your favs.

A lot of affirmative work is self-referential, and it can become cyclical in a rather Uroboros, the serpent that devours itself, sort of way. If you can only talk about what exists in the canon and only the creator/s can add to that canon then there is a worry that the fandom might stagnate until more content is forthcoming. Fans can get stuck in a certain way of thinking about the canon, the narrative and characters because there are only the creator's ideas to reference from, or the ideas of a small sub-set of 'valid' critics to take from.

For the most part affirmative fandom rolls with the punches though and it is a very enjoyable way of bringing what you love into your life. Having a collection of merchandise, official or fan-made, of your favourite clone from *Star Wars* or *My Little Pony* character is a way of showing your connection to them and that franchise, as is doing a deep dive into the in-game history of *Five Nights At Freddy's* and posting a two-hour long video on YouTube. I have watched more mockumentary, video game deep dives than I care to admit and it is worth it every time; it's fun, silly and ultimately enjoyable whilst being educational. If learning about how killer robots in an indie horror game work can be called educational.

It boils down to being a way that some, if not all, fans want to engage with fandom at one point or another. Almost everyone collects, almost everyone has meta that they may or may not share with the wider world, almost everyone likes to go to a panel or talk from time to time, or queue up to get a signed picture. All well and good.

It is worth noting, and this is a generalisation so take it with a pinch of salt, that many of the fans who favour affirmative styles of fandom are guys, and often they are the guys who get to see themselves represented well in the canon most of the time. For them, there really isn't anything that needs to be changed or transformed within the canon so engaging with it as is works for them because they are the lead, so why transform any of it?

In the original meta essay discussing the two forms of fandom that were being seen by obsession_inc they state, in relation to affirmational fandom that: '...I would argue, the majority of fans that trend strongly toward affirmational fannish activities are male.'

While there is no reason for any form of fandom to be gendered, exclusive or feel exclusionary, this is something that comes up time and time again. In the introduction you were asked to picture a fan and that idea of the fanboy in his bedroom, *The Big Bang Theory* nerd stereotype and all that came with it will probably have flashed into your mind. The image of the fanboy is affirmative, largely due to them being catered for by the media that we consume at all times. No matter what you're a fan of, there's a likelihood that male protagonists are pretty much at the centre of it all with anyone else often seeing themselves as a tokenistic side character at best or a 2-D cardboard cut-out to be seen as joke, a sex object or just die within the first minute at best.

And if that's the case, there is possibly a reason why many folks, particularly women, queer people, people of colour and other minority groups, who never get to see themselves represented in a particularly favourable way, turn to making their own versions of them.

Transformative – Fanart, Fanfiction, etc.

Look, if you didn't have a *Sonic* 'sona' (not that we called them that, all those moons ago when I was young) when you were a kid then have you really lived in fandom? Or were you more of the *Warrior Cats* generation? Whatever it was there is a certain sort of collective fandom memory that definitely makes us all inwardly cringe a little at how bad we might see them as now, but at least it's a shared cringe experience. And not one we should be all that ashamed of either.

One of the biggest parts of fandom is creating your own works, characters and stories around what has been put down in canon. Love it or hate it you cannot deny that it is there and that lots of people find an amazing form or self-expression through it.

What you maybe don't know is what exactly counts as transformative works under the definitions that we are carving our way through. It's easy to say that it's the opposite of affirmative, but there's a bit – a lot – more to it than that.

In basic terms, Transformative Fandom is works that add to, change, challenge or open up the canon narrative in some way. This is your fanart, fan videos, role playing, and fanfiction. It is most often engaged with or made by people who don't tend to see themselves as the leads in media and are looking for ways to relate to the characters in the stories or to add people like themselves into them.

The big things that you will see in transformative works are gender-changing, race-changing and slash fiction to add a queer narrative to a piece of media that may or may not have been teased in the text in some way. People are looking to find themselves in a sea of characters that are only one or two types of people, and so they take the dolls themselves and play their own way.

But it's not just that.

Transformative Fandom is one of the two types of fandom that is defined within fan studies and fan spaces... This can even include making creations with crochet, filming fan-films for YouTube, or making music about your favourite video games. It's fans finding new and creative ways to play around with canon, however they see fit.

Transformative Fandom takes that element of self-identity and making your fandom part of who you are and pushes it as far as it can go. Every day there is a new transformative style being developed and experimented with. Any type of creative art can have a fan twist on it and that allows for not only that self-expression and journey of identity that people have through fandom but also it stops fan cultures and the works that inspire them from stagnating.

If all you have are those self-referential works then people may drift off from fan or community spaces in favour of other things, or negative feeling can develop in the spaces due to the lack of newest. But if you have a constant stream of new fics, cool art, alternative universes (AUs), music videos, etc, then your fandom can be self-fulfilling to the end of time. What all these works do is create a literal multiverse from the original canon.

Every coffee shop AU, every fix-it fic, every race-changed piece of art, all of it is just the story gone down another trouser leg of time and playing out in some other universe. This means that somewhere out there is an omegaverse for everything and, make of that what you will.

With all these different spider webs of canon, there are times when something a little odd happens. Something you wouldn't necessarily think of. All these AUs and fanworks can lead to people becoming fans of the fandom ideas rather than the original piece of media, particularly if there is a huge multiverse of versions that are all their own, unique thing that have been created along the way.

Each new transformative work adds a new piece of fandom for fans to engage with. The more works you have, the easier it is to get new people interested. The more people are interested, the more new works you get.

You like an artist, they get into a new podcast or video game and you are suddenly consuming their fanworks of that thing that was never the thing you started liking them for in the first place. Doesn't mean that you'll become a die-hard fan of the podcast or video game but it opens the door to you.

The wider you spread the multiverse of ideas that are coming out of all the fans' heads, the more likely you are to find people who may never have considered this fandom to be of interest to them and thus stagnation is avoided.

This is not to say that transformative works are better than affirmative works, you need both to build fandom. Both have a place and both give fans a different view point and understanding of not only the original piece of media but the other fans around them. There are just as many issues with people only engaging with the transformed works and possibly not even watching/reading/playing the original piece of media as there are with not seeing the transformed works as valid as the canon. Humans be humaning after all, can't escape that, so it's important that we don't see them as opposing but as two sides of a very nerdy coin.

Ships Ahoy!

'You know what? I really think those two characters should hold hands.'
 'What? But that character is in a relationship with someone else in canon!'
 'Well, they have two hands, don't they?'

If you have spent any amount of time in fandom spaces the likelihood of you hearing or seeing a conversation somewhere along these lines is pretty high. Shipping – relationshipping – has made its way into pretty much every type of fandom under the sun, yes, even ones for real people.

Author note: I once had the misfortune of stumbling across fanfiction written about politicians and, let me tell you, there were some interesting ideas about the Liberal Democrats that I have never been able to unknow.

The act of shipping two, or more, characters in a way that isn't necessarily part of the canon is super common in fandom spaces. It's definitely one of the things that people outside of fandom seem to be most aware of. It has rather breached containment in that regard. But why is it so much a part of the fan experience to want to write, draw, or generally engage with shipping? What is there to gain from it if it hasn't been fulfilled in the original canon?

Other than the obvious, which I don't think I need to go into, there is a reason that people know about shipping fics and art, and shipping can be wanted by fans for any number of reasons. Be it that relationships in canon felt forced and they want to fix them, that they personally relate to a different character so want to see their relationship with the lead or someone else play out differently, or they might want to see a close friendship develop into something else; there's plenty of reasons, but it all comes back to one thing really: inclusion and exploration.

Okay, that's two things but they go hand in hand, just like Kirk and Spock.

We are right back at that need to see yourself, particularly for young, questioning people who are uncertain about all the interesting, and maybe worrisome, changes and feelings that make themselves known in your teens and twenties. Even into your later life – I hesitate to call thirties later life because there is a world after twenty-five – the need for a space to discover ideas about your own wants, needs and preferences in relationships at every possible level is a very prominent one. Look at how many romance novels and bodice rippers there are out there, it's the same type of thing. There's been more than a few fanfictions that have made their way onto the bestsellers list once they've had make-over and a new name attached.

With shipping though you don't have to worry about what is going to make its way through a publisher to the bookshop, you can make up your own story as you go, playing pick and mix with the characters you love and the ways they interact.

Shipping particularly allows for LGBTQIA+ people looking to explore and understand their own sexuality to do so in relative safety and privacy. It is a very personal journey, coming to terms with your own sexuality, and creating or viewing queer relationships has, up until very recently, been an uphill struggle, if not nigh on impossible. One of the only places people were able to find to explore ideas of sexuality was in shipping and reading fanfiction. It's safe, it's fictional, you can be completely anonymous, it's free, all of that means you can read it without anyone knowing if needs be. The same is true of fanart, though text on a screen is much less obvious than brightly coloured or large-scale pieces of artwork.

The same need for exploration around sexuality and attraction can be seen in the 'your name' or self-insert style fics. These are either written specifically for the writer to see themselves in the world of the fandom with their fav, or to allow the reader to do that by putting 'your name' in the space of the protagonist of the fic with whichever character it is about. These fics will often specify the gender of the 'your name' character, with there sometimes being variations of the fic for different genders in order for a more well-rounded experience for the reader.

A lot of fanfiction readers and writers are young people, often young women, though not exclusively by any stretch of the imagination, who are looking for ways to experiment, learn and understand about themselves in a completely safe way. Shipping in some way can provide that be they straight, questioning or part of the LGBTQIA+ community.

While there is an argument to be made that a lot of the male/male (slash) character ships stem from the lack of well written female characters in media – again, something that is changing – there is also plenty to be said for 'playing dolls' with fictional characters who you relate to regardless of gender. And there is a strong, and ever growing, number of female/female (femmeslash) character ships as well.

To quote physiologist Dr Lynn Zubernis, cited in the article *The Sweet Science of Shipping* by Maggie Owens on Fandom.com:

> 'It's all about identity exploration. We're all going around looking for depictions of our own romantic, sexual, and emotional fantasies. Shipping is a self-narrative therapy.'

All Together Now

I am sat in the Tate Archives without a cup of tea. This is the closest I have ever felt to being a 'real' academic and it's absolutely freezing. Turns out it being one of the hottest days of the year does not change the need for archives to be kept cool or the fact that you really shouldn't have tea near an archive. I had not factored this in. It doesn't matter though because I am looking at a pile of 'zines and golly, it's exciting.

Not one of them is some holy grail of 'zines, but seeing these few 'zines from the collection, that span three decades and several different fandoms, is exciting because they are unique. These are from small runs, made for groups of friends or fan communities, and most have been squirreled away or possibly just lost and gone over time. Getting to see them, photocopied, stapled together and hand-made, is a delight.

Each one contains some art, some fiction, quotes and a meta essay. You can feel the hands of the fans who added to them and those who curated them just by holding one of these small documents in your own hand. And you can see the different types of fandom at work in them and blended together.

Okay, there's been a lot of talk about 'zines already, but they hold a special place not just in fandom but in sub-cultures across the board. They are a collective work to celebrate and discuss and openly congregate together in a single body of work, drawing all the strings of a sub-culture or fandom together. They are, in many ways, a point for Affirmative and Transformative Fandom to join together.

A 'zine, in itself, is something that people collect, and may end up in archives like the Tate or one of the many 'zine libraries around the world – if you ever get a chance to visit one, please do and consider donating any 'zines of your own, it's important to preserve them. It can be a piece of affirmative fandom history, documenting what fans were like before your time. It may have collected together bodies of work into an archival document to be shared and inform other fans of opinions, possibly even the opinions of actors or creators who add themselves into a 'zine project. This is what 'zines, right back to the earliest fan clubs were for.

But 'zines are transformative themselves because they are made by fans to add to the canon in some way, whilst also containing transformative works. Experimental works, works that could only be shared with safe people at one point, works that started a revolution in how we think and talk in fan spaces, and works that didn't but are no less important as a piece of fan expression.

Pretty heavy lifting for printer paper and staples.

It's hard not to see them as something special though. Folk history you could call it, the inner lives and ideas of the everyday person, of fans, alt-fashion and culture lovers, political activists and conversationalists all wrapped up in this one style of publication, often all in one single 'zine in fact, produced for and by themselves. It's worth sitting in the cold without caffeine to look at them.

Fan-driven projects like 'zines are the reason why a lot of this history isn't lost. Building projects about what inspires us as a community, particularly in fan and sub-cultural spaces where different styles of working can be pulled into these projects, it gives a window into a moment of unity and understanding between individuals. Sometimes it shows you what happens when things don't work out, but that's pretty fun to see too. Who doesn't like getting to look at drama you aren't involved in?

They are an alternative history as much as they are affirmative and transformative works. Knowing that Marvel Studios grossed the box office with first weekend ticket sales of the latest superhero blockbuster on whatever date is one thing, knowing how fans of side character number six who got their first on-screen appearance in two years is another. And having it recorded in a way that won't vanish when Elon Musk shuts down Twitter for good, or there's a digital fanfiction purge, has an importance that cannot be over-stated. You spend so much time with this piece of media and these people, of course the natural thing is to want to share that with each other and others who can be brought into the fold. Look, some of us just like to lurk and feel included when they pre-order a 'zine or sponsor a fan kickstarter project.

But 'zines aren't the only outlier in all this. I know, I'm shocked too. Two categories aren't enough to lock down everything about a sub-culture? Honestly, what is the world coming to when we can't look at things in the binary? While 'zines are good example of how a point of crossover can work between the two 'factions' of fandom, by their very nature they can only allow for mediums that work in print – digital 'zines can be an exception to this rule because nothing is ever hard and fast – so there's a whole world of fanworks and fannish behaviours that just don't get a look in here. And some of them, well, they really know how to blur a line out of existence.

Above: The comic book store from TV show *The Big Bang Theory* from The Comic Centre of Pasadena, a perfect example of affirmative style fandom. By Chester, Creative Commons BY 2.0.

Left: Anime books collected and displayed in Kyoto, Japan by Marek Slusarczyk, Creative Commons BY 3.0.

Fans looking for merchandise at Gamescom 2018, by Tim Bartel, Creative Commons BY-SA 2.0.

Collectors' items at MCM London, by Big-Ashb, Creative Commons BY 2.0.

Transformative fanart of *Marvel Comic's* canonical couple Shatterstar and Rictor, by David Wynne.

Above and overleaf: Transformative fanart of *Marvel Comic's* ever so slightly less (ie not at all) canonical couple Iron Man and Captain America, by David Wynne.

Above, below and overleaf pages: Images from a fandom crafting workshop by Alasdair Watson Photography in Glasgow.

2 Performance as a Fanwork

How many of you have seen a cosplayer, or a pack of cosplayers, standing outside a convention in the best spot they can find, striking a pose and snapping photos of each other? Or perhaps listened to a podcast getting to the bottom of a plot hole in the latest episode of *Doctor Who*? Would you call these things fanworks? Or performances?

Cosplay, podcasts, fan-music and fan-films are just a few of the better known types of performance-based fandom that make their way around the fan sphere, becoming more or less popular in the natural ebb and flow of these things. Though in the last few years, the tide seems to be permanently coming in for these styles of fanwork and, pushing the metaphor a bit far, they are flooding the scene. Cosplay has definitely found its feet under the big kids' table with fanfic and fanart, but that doesn't mean it's all that well understood as its own thing, and the others are still finding ways to be part of the club in a big way.

The thing with performance-based fan works is that it's pretty hard to put them into the general boxes that we've just come to think of as the two pillars of fan interaction. You'd think that cosplay or making music was transformative by its very nature – you aren't the original actor/character/setting but if you are pushing to recreate something faultlessly you are referring back to the affirmative in order to create screen accuracy or a picture-perfect expression of the original. It depends on each creator where they fall rather than the medium or genre of fanwork as a collective. There are so many arguments either way.

All of these styles of fanwork blur the edges of where stories start and the fandom ends. It also leads to fan-creators being creators in their own right, with fandoms of their own interested in their works because they are making works of things they like while introducing them to new things as well. It is not all that unusual for this to become a thing with fanartists or even fic writers, but it's a much more obvious blurred line with creators who work in a more performance-based art form.

You're putting your face, your name, your personality on the label when you put that work out there. You have to in many cases because you're literally using your body to make the art. Performative fanworks tend to end up being their own sub-cultures, a sub-culture inside a sub-culture inside a sub-culture. Think about it as very nerdy stacking dolls, just with something a little more on the geeky side at the core.

Let's crack open the onion and delve into its layers to see what sort of fanworks are hiding in its murky depth and what they are changing in their own way.

If Music be the Food of Fandom, Play On

When I say 'nerd music' your mind probably jumps to electro like Daft Punk's *Tron Legacy* soundtrack or maybe video game style music, or perhaps film, TV and game scores in general. That sort of thing. Maybe there was novelty track in there, Doctoring the TARDIS or Leonard Nimoy's song about *The Hobbit*. There's a lot out there that might well spring to mind, but what about music written specifically by fans for their fandoms, not in an attempt for novelty, rather serious pieces of art that just so happen to be about nerd stuff? And maybe also give you a chuckle if you get a reference or two? Not your thing? Good reader, you are missing out.

I have been waiting on Zoom for a meeting, for a little while now. This is a meeting with someone who I am little nervous about talking to. They are someone who makes some of the most iconic, in my opinion, original fandom-based works around. And I'm a big fan of what they do. It's a strange feeling to be nervous to talk to a fellow fan but it is what it is. Another five minutes and slightly panicked 'Oh no, I overslept!' message, and here they are. Flashing up onto the screen, inside their recording studio that is looking much more professional than my own office mic, and with a coffee in hand.

This is The Stupendium, aka Greg Holgate, a nerdcore artist who has taken the gaming community by storm in recent years with their clever word play, impeccable rap and catchy melodies with songs all revolving around games. While they are very definitely original pieces, each one is also a fanwork in its own right, often with Greg's own additional character ideas, set in the world of the game, looking at the larger world and adding to it as new piece of media. Some focus on a character(s) or the central of the plot of the game, others take a much broader point of view, but all are excellent, and my goodness can they make you want to jump in and play right alongside Greg, and other nerdcore artists like them.

Nerdcore, for those who might not know, is part of a sub-set of fan creators whose art is not pen on paper or digital comics, but musical. If you were a SuperWhoLock fan in the late '00s, early '10s – I was there, the day the strength of fans failed – you would have known about a whole span of music about all three of these fandoms, as well as them collectively. And they were not alone in this. Pretty much every major, and minor, online fandom has had someone making music about it if you look hard enough. And this is nerdcore.

Nowadays the term tends to be more connected with anime, manga and video games, with stylistic leanings to rap, hip-pop and techno. You might see fandoms giving their own little group of songs/artists a collective name such as Trock for Timelord Rock in *Doctor Who* or Wizard Rock for the *Harry Potter* fandom, both of which were very popular around the early to mid-2010s, but mostly it all comes under the single banner of nerdcore today.

It goes back well before the internet, of course, but with YouTube entering the fray with its user-friendly interface for both media consumer and creator and the rise of easy access online music creation programmes, it is unsurprising that this genre of fanworks has been given an injection of life that sent it into the spaces usually held by the more mainstream styles of works.

You didn't have to be able to play an instrument or even be a trained singer any more with these programmes, nor did you have to have a fancy set-up to record. If fanfic and fanart are popular because they are accessible, that's what these programmes did for the fan-music side of things. You could suddenly do it all without having to break the bank.

> 'Any art form is intimidating,' Greg says adjusting the camera slightly, 'when you're looking at it from an outside perspective, as somebody who wants to get into it. I remember being a *Sonic the Hedgehog* fan artist age thirteen (author note: I told you so), and drawing my terrible little things and looking at these incredible artists on TV, and I'm thinking, why even try these, I'm never going to get that good. So, I think there's that sort of intimidation getting into any of it. But music particularly does have that very, very technical skill set. Like it's something that's harder to just learn already, I guess, these days of the laptop, not so much.
>
> I've become aware of small channels trying to make their way in music, mostly, you know, in the anime rap or rap scene, but in general, I feel like there's a lot more small channels starting out, learning as they go. So, I think hopefully, those barriers are coming down over time.'

Encouraging more people into finding a form of fanwork that fits them, that doesn't just have to be in what is traditionally seen as the transformative or the affirmative ways of doing things, keeps fandom exciting. It might all come back to the same root idea or need; finding the way to interact with what you love in your own way can be just as formative as the media itself. It might not even be the first thing that springs to mind that enthuses you, or the thing you've 'trained' in that carries your creativity forwards.

Which is something that is interesting about Greg, they aren't a musician in the traditional way of things at all, they are an animator.

'I came into it from a very different angle to I feel like everyone else in nerdcore because I was a fan of it for years of growing up a quite a small part of it. There were just a few artists that I was aware of that I really liked: Dan Bull being the main one, JT music another one. I listened to it for years.'

These are both two people who Greg now collaborates with, and definitely names in nerdcore that have made their way out of this slightly niche-r scene into the wider fan community at large and beyond. It's just really good music whether it's about *Minecraft* or not.

'I sort of wrote stuff in my spare time as a hobby lyrically, not necessarily all nerdcore stuff, just songs and poetry, and I'd been making YouTube for a long time, none of [what they were doing] was really working, so I thought, I'm going to do a song. It's nothing I've done before but I'm going to have a go. I'd worked in video animation for five, six, seven, eight years, had a degree in that, so I thought, "I'm going to pour everything I've got into it; I'm going to animate a full music video for a nerdcore song. And if it does well, then I'll stay on YouTube. If it doesn't, I'm going to move on and find a new hobby." I poured like 18 months into making this one nerdcore song, "Find the Keys", about *Bendy and the Ink Machine*. And it just, it just went viral. And it completely blew up.'

Author note: It is a hell of a video, and it is worth watching if you aren't already into this genre of music, or even if you are and could do with a nice little pick-me-up on a rainy day. Guaranteed to make your brain tingle.

'That sort of cemented my fate,' they say with a shrug and a laugh, 'and then I found myself playing catch up. Because I don't have any real formal musical training. I'm all in video. And everyone else in nerdcore seems to be people who've trained in music for a long time and had to either work out the video or hire video editors. I'm the complete opposite.'

Greg isn't alone in this. Finding a way into different types of fanwork creation, with skills that don't feel like the obvious choice for the work at hand, isn't a bad thing. If you want to add something to the growing field of works in your community or want to find an artistic avenue to express your love for fandom in some way, that need to learn and evolve the skills you have in different, unexpected ways gives you a push as creator to innovate. That's how fandoms and pop culture get bigger and better, not because everyone does the same thing all the same. That is what makes nerdcore as a style of fanworks stand out. It definitely sets The Stupendium apart with the way the videos feel.

The animation, consideration for costume and set design, and overall production values that Greg brings to each video, give the songs an edge so that you don't just want to listen, you want to experience. Add into that mix the fact that Greg themself may not be a musician but they have writing skills that would put the best lyricists and rappers in the music industry to shame.

Each nerdcore artist brings their own take on the medium to the table. Where one may have strengths in rap, another may be a melodic genius, another a whizz with as many different instruments as you can throw at them, one can form full narrative structure, another might hit deep to the heart of a character. There's so much to take from each individual creator it's not hard to start getting excited to see what they do next. It's even more exciting when they collaborate together. Ed Sheeran and all his collaborations are nothing to a nerdcore cypher – according to Google a cypher 'is a gathering of rappers, beatboxers, and/or breakers in a circle, extemporaneously making music together'.

All of this leads to recipe of a style of fanwork that goes above and beyond, but also does something else. It starts to generate a fandom of its very own.

I am a fan of The Stupendium, but I'm not necessarily a fan of every piece of media that they have covered in their songs, and this is the case for many fans of nerdcore. They get hooked in by something that does enter into their fan-sphere – in my own case it was due to one of their songs being used heavily on Tiktok videos in a fandom I was part of – and then follow the path of enjoying the creator as an artist in their own right. I became a fan of a fandom creator, not of single fandom itself. This is very, very common with creators in this more performative area of fanworks, it happens with cosplayers too. The personality of the creator shines through their works in a way that you as the audience can connect to, so when they move onto another topic you go with them rather than scrolling past or clicking away, which can often happen with more traditional styles of fanwork on both sides of the fandom coin.

With Greg's background as an animator, this allowed them to stand out as well as giving them the space to build The Stupedium 'persona' around their animations as they improved their musical ability and tapped into a pre-existing fan-base for games like *Bendy and the Ink Machine* that are looking for new ways to be fans.

If you look at it nerdcore music is, at its heart, a form of fanfiction. Both of these types of fanwork, alongside works like fan-comics and fan-cam videos, in some way hit the same beats, let's call them. You take characters, a world, a story and retell or add to that fandom element with a story or reframing of your own as a fan. You do that in the medium of your choice: writing, drawing, maybe knitting, or, in this case, music. Within nerdcore this can swing from being a straight, musical version of the original media thus changing medium to create a new type of content, it could be blending medias e.g. *Doctor Who* doing the Time Warp from *Rocky Horror* – one for the old school Tumblr fans of the Hillywood videos – or it could be a changing the focus onto a different character, building on the world in some way or creating an AU. There any number of things you can do within the medium not limited to, or excluding, rap battles.

Who would have guessed that the argument between who would win, Batman or Superman, is more fun when done in lyrical rhyme and take downs rather than a Reddit thread. It's creating new ways to look at old ideas and having an unusual way of coming at it that refreshes whole fandoms and adds to the fandom building around the creator themselves by drawing in new fans from all over.

When it comes to their own work, Greg has their own certain way of approaching all this; creating a story within the existing world of the media that is being nerdcore-d – yeah, I read it back. I'm sticking with it.

It feels more akin to tabletop roleplaying storytelling, new characters within an existing world, and that only adds to the interest when they, and other nerdcore artists, release something new. You never quite know what you are going to get.

'Focusing on trying to try and make all my content feel like it legitimately is from the world of the game. That is a big part of why what I try and do.' And that is obvious – whichever of their videos you pick, you'll find that Greg has buried themselves in lore, through the music, the aesthetics, the lyrical twists and turns in such a way that you feel dropped into the piece of media without a second thought. 'I'm not interested in saying, and here's a song about when first I met this character from Undertale, and this character, and then beat the boss, that you've played the game, you know, that story has no interest in me for just retelling.'

The line between fan and creator is a thin one, that is easily and often crossed. Nerdcore isn't the only area of fandom that it happens in, but it is one of the more obvious for fan-creators building up their own fanbases around fanworks rather than having to make the changes that fic writers or artists have to or making the move into original pieces that is often the path that people take.

More and more fans are exploring the boundaries of what being a fan means. For many that means pushing against the framework of fandom styles, the categories that have played a large part in fan studies for the last decade, and deciding for themselves where they see their works sitting, or if they even sit inside those categories at all. For others that means being like Greg and other fan creators and becoming a part of the media of the fandom in their own right. But for some, this isn't quite enough. The fourth walls need to come down so you can start getting inside the whole thing.

Costume to Tell the Story

Okay, we got through three, maybe three and half of our questions. I behaved myself. Now we get to talk about cosplay.

I never thought that I would be putting myself so much in to this book. It took me a little bit by surprise suddenly finding myself so deeply connected with all the fans that I spoke with, understanding their stories through my own experience and presenting them alongside each other, but really, I should have seen that coming from the start. Because I love cosplay. It's one of the more elaborate forms of fanwork and means putting yourself into the shoes of the characters, fandoms and stories that you love in the most personal way possible. You become them.

Here's me doing that with this book. That might sound a touch on the strange side but hear me out.

Cosplay opens up a whole world of ideas around making your fandom part of who you are. It's extreme, really, to be putting yourself so inside a character that you personify them entirely for a time. It's blending the two, fan and the media, together to the point that they can't be separated because they are literally one thing.

If you don't know what cosplay is, and I would be amazed at this point if you didn't since it appears, in recent years, to be taking the world, if not by storm, then definitely by squall… or cloud (this is a very bad joke about *Final Fantasy*, the first fandom that I cosplayed from. I apologise).

Cosplay is short for 'costume play', a term coined in the 1980s by a Japanese journalist after seeing people dressing up at World Con. It is essentially the act of dressing up as a character, item, or thing, from popular culture.

The hobby dates back at least to the 1930s, but there are strong arguments for it making its first technical appearance right back into the late 1800s. But since humans have always liked dressing up and playing make-believe, it, much like fandom, is rather hard to pin down. If you are interested in more about cosplay check out *A Guide to Film and TV Cosplay* and the sequel *A Guide to Anime, Manga and Video Game Cosplay* both by me. Shameless plug over.

Okay? Good. Let's continue.

You would think that by the very nature of cosplay that it would have to be 'transformative', right? You literally transform yourself when you put on the costume, but because there are multiple ways of approaching the same thing with a cosplay it can also fall into the 'affirmative'.

If you are the type of fan who loves canon, creating works that uphold it, and affirming it for yourself and others, you are likely to be making 100 per cent screen/panel accurate costumes for yourself and that is going to be the type of cosplay that you take pleasure in being the audience for as well. Because of course, cosplay is a performance and therefore has an audience, but we will get to that later.

Cosplayers like this might join groups like the 501st, a *Star Wars* cosplay group famous, or possibly infamous, for the levels of accuracy it requires to join. This is the way that you are having fun, with other people who are having fun in that way. You affirm each other, you affirm the canon, you are still a cosplayer.

And there are loads of people who love this style of cosplay, doing everything they can to reach an almost look-a-like quality with their work. Hunting down all the details, 3-D printing pieces to get the exact belt buckle, or learning a brand new skill just so they can make a garment true to screen. It can be a really fun challenge to undertake.

The flip side to this is the 'transformative'.

It is a little bit harder to define, there is a lot of variation from cosplayer to cosplayer how they approach their own work, so while some will be very obvious in their transformational elements, modifying or completely redesigning a character for example, or even cosplaying as something like the game of *Tetris,* with others you may not be able to point it out as obviously. The literal, physical changes and transformations to the appearance of the character being cosplayed aren't anywhere near as transformative as the act of putting it on your own body and taking a claim of the character, their story and the fandom at large in your own way by doing so. It is that element of it being put onto the body of an individual and them putting as much or as little of themselves into the work and the performance as they want that tips a costume into an affirmative or transformative space in the fan-sphere.

See, both. Or neither? Or moving between the two depending on the individual in question? Difficult.

Cosplay is an incredibly personal form of fanwork, you can't escape the fact that you are making yourself, your physical body and everything that comes with that, part of the work. It slaps a big label on your head that you are a fan of this thing and you are putting your own identity out there as such.

This is where the audience comes in.

If you are reading a fanfiction, or watching a deep dive video essay into canon, you pretty much know what you are going to get with the style of fanwork you are engaging with. You tend not to stumble onto a style of fanwork you aren't that keen on as they tend to exist in different spaces, either as literal different websites or 'zines; through your own curation of your space; or through online algorithms working out what you like and giving you more of that. With cosplay, that's a little different. You can like and engage with purely screen accurate cosplays, but since that's not all that cosplay is you will also have to engage with, and be the audience of, other types of cosplays because they inhabit the same space, both literally and metaphorically.

You can't go to Comic Con and only see the 501st.

This means that the audience of cosplay is adding to whether it is seen as affirmative or transformative with the way that they interact with it. If you see someone saying 'this is canon *Sailor Moon*' they are adding to the levels of affirmation around that cosplay, but if you see 'this is such a cool take on the character, so original', that is adding to the transformational. You might also see some very negative comments about not being 'good' enough to be the character in some way, which is the audience trying to push the affirmative onto a cosplayer regardless of what they themselves might be trying to achieve.

But does this mean that the audience are the ones placing a category on the cosplay, or is it up to the cosplayer to decide? Well, it's both. You can't have a performance without an audience now, can you? It can lead to crossed wires of what the cosplayer is trying to achieve vs what the audience, or members of the audience, are taking from it, but you can't stop that. For the most part the costume and whatever level of performance is attached to it, will speak for itself.

The audience aside, the way that cosplayers choose to perform their characters differs from person to person and from performative medium to performative medium. It's not just putting on a costume and hanging out with your mates, you know.

Cosplay competition skits, music videos, fan-films and photographs, where cosplayers completely take on the role of the character within a performance space are super popular with both the cosplayers themselves and wider fandoms at large. These are different types of performance than simply wearing your costume or observing cosplayers on the convention hall. It goes a step deeper by literally attempting to become and portray the character as authentically as possible from the point of view of that cosplayer or group of cosplayers and putting it out there for others to view. The place where media and fan meet once again becomes more intertwined.

Fourth wall, whomst?

When you look at the transformative and the affirmative here, you can see the two in some very obvious ways. Taking videos and photographs at conventions or meets is a big part of cosplay. It blurs the line between the person and the character in a dramatic way simply by showing the cosplayers in the space of the event and thus setting them as people dressing up as the characters. This is very clearly a transformative work in many ways, rather than say in a stage set or studio, or on a specialised location where you are trying to emulate the characters and media in as much detail as humanly possible.

This gives two slightly different styles of performance and identity creation around the cosplay and the cosplayer, but neither is set in stone as both can be playing with elements of transformation and affirmation of the original fandom media.

This is also allows for other types of fanworks to be made by non-cosplayers, the ones making the videos or taking the pictures. They are part of making the cosplay come to life and add to its place within both categories of fandom whilst also making a brand new, completely separate piece of fanwork of their own celebrating those characters that they love and the cosplayers who are wearing them.

This has gotten very deep. Did I mention it was a special point of interest for me?

Essentially cosplay manages to muddle up the whole idea that there's two type of fandom by adding in an unquestionable human element. You cannot simply remove the cosplayer from the costume, you see their choices, their fandom preferences, their own ideas about the character and their story, their way of interacting with the fandom in how they have gone about turning themselves into what they love. You see it again in the way that they portray themselves in photos and videos then with the added element of how the person behind the camera is interacting with fandom, if they want to make something that shows the person inside the costume or the costume as the major element over the person. And then you add the audience viewing all of this into that and phew! It's a bit of a muddle of everything.

Where 'zines calmly collect everything together into one place to be viewed as a work of its own that embodies many types of fandom, cosplay is the chaotic fandom sibling being everything all at once and changing radically depending on the individual involved and the point at which they start to interact with the cosplay.

So, try to define this one if you dare, fan studiers. Cosplay might just have broken the system, or at least given us all something to get our teeth into. But I'll admit, even for me that was a lot. Time for a cuppa and nice sit down me thinks, maybe blow off some steam.

You up for some tabletop games?

Greg 'The Stupendium' Holgate.

YouTube thumbnails of some of The Stupendium's greatest hits.

Above and overleaf pages: Cosplayers rocking it as Chompette, Boosette and Bowsette from *Super Mario,* designed by themselves, photos taken by Megaera Amis.

Meggo Photo

Above left, above right and left: Cosplayers Spider-Punk, Peter B. Parker and Spider Gwen from *Into The Spiderverse* showing off how many versions of one character there really are! Photos take by Megaera Amis.

Above and below: Videography and photography ParsleyLeaves YouTube title cards, bringing cosplay to life on the digital screen.

3 Roll For Initiative: Tabletop Roleplaying Games

It comes to the understanding of this author that some people may never have played a Tabletop Roleplaying Game (TTRPG), or at least not knowingly done so, they can be sneaky buggers. No, they aren't boardgames... sometimes they can have a board though, and they are sold in the same section, so you would be forgiven for thinking they are the same. And also no, they aren't the same thing as Roleplaying (RPG) video games. There is a definite crossover between all these things, but what a TTRPG is, that's very much its own, well, a lot bigger and more unwieldy beast. You'd be more likely to down an ancient dragon at level five than get your head around a tabletop roleplaying game in your first session.

TTRPG is a catch-all term for roleplaying systems, led by a Dungeon Master (DM) – get your head out of the gutter – or Games Master (GM) in which the players design their own characters from of a set of ability classes, fantastical or sci-fi species, story backgrounds and/or character traits (other variations of this are available but you get the idea) with more or less of their own creativity depending on the player. Together the players will then tell a story guided by the GM, that may or may not be massively derailed by the players deciding to do stuff counter to the GM's plans. This can be in either a pre-made adventure setting and story created by the publishers of the game rules, or in a world of their own using the game rules as a starting point for designing their own set-up and adventure. And, of course, there are plenty of happy medium places for your group to fall into.

It can be more, or less, complex depending on the play system you are using; some have hundreds of rules, books and books and, oh yes, more books full of rules, stats and anything else you might desire that add onto the original ones that are already pretty long, or they may only have a page or so of rules for easier access for newcomers to the play style.

Summed up, it's communal storytelling. You save the world with your friends or end it if that's more your gig. It can span years, or just a single day, but in more cases than not it's an intense experience where life-long friendships are forged and where no one outside of your party ever knows what you did. But you know and that's what import.

Sounds super fun, right? Good, because it totally is and definitely worth doing. But why is it being brought up in a book about fandom?

Good question. Honestly, you readers, you really do ask the perfect questions to get the right information, it's great.

TTRPGs are the middle ground. Where fanworks might confuse or collect differing types of fandom, TTRPGs wrap them up together in a neat bag of holding for you to pick out at your leisure. Harmony brought about by violent, magical chaos.

Unlike other types of media, including other gaming media such as video games, on the whole, TTRPGs have a lot more scope for change and creativity. Whilst still having their own canons, stories and rule sets to pay by, with these games, as long as the other players and your Game Master are cool with it, you can mess around the canon of the rulebooks as much as you want but you are still playing the TTRPG and not making a fanwork outside of the media.

Change the canon. Make up your own worlds using the rules systems. Heck, change the rules – if it's cool you can do it. Or you can all play exactly how it's meant to be played with no changes at all whatsoever. It's all valid as part of the game.

But here's the thing, it doesn't matter how much you deviate or not, you are still making your own version of the TTRPG simply by playing it. You will all tell the story that bit differently, can't be helped. You're all doing it together, with the characters you made, who have their own stories to weave and who you all are likely to get pretty invested in as you tell the tale. You're making the multiverse in the same way as fanfiction and fanart no matter how fiercely you stick to the rules.

Clever that, isn't it?

The other brilliantly fannish behaviour with TTRPGs is how quickly you become fans of each other's characters. If I counted the number of times I'd been in a game where people ended up making art of some sort about the members of the party I would have quite a few of my toes left to count but all my fingers would have been used up.

It's not just art of each other's characters either. Groups will cosplay their characters together, they might write fics based around their own games, some players really like making battle set ups and miniatures to make it all the more fun to play together. It's not uncommon for players to have dice, counters and other knickknacks to match their character, and not just one character either. They are likely to have all that for each character they play in each game and people will gift each other add-ons for their character set-up. It's a big thing.

All of this though is made even more interesting when you throw live play shows online into the mix.

Streamed or recorded 'live play' shows are one of the hottest tickets in pop culture at the moment. The most famous of them is *Critical Role* which started back in 2015 and steadily built an audience of fans watching the adventures of the characters as well as becoming fans of the players themselves. It is a multi-faceted fan experience. *Critical Role* and its contemporaries such as *The Adventure Zone* and *Dimension 20*, all approach the games in very individual ways to create unique experiences for the players and the fans alike and this has led to some of the fastest growing fandoms, and some of the most interesting and entertaining fanworks in recent years.

So, if you're a fan of the shows, are you a fan of TTRPGs or are you a fan of the players, or are you a fan of the characters and the story? All of the above?

Much like with becoming a fan of a fan-creator, there's levels to all this that build different fandoms around the same thing. Lots of people are fans of TTRPGs without ever watching a live play game, and visa versa. People cosplay from *Critical Role* and are part of the 'Critter' community, they may even design their own characters to exist within the world of *Critical Role* but they aren't actually playing the game. Whilst other people will never do more than stick to what's laid down in the books, both these people could well be considered fans of the same thing.

The thing with all this is that you can take any TTRPG and you can look at it as piece of media with an affirmative fandom or a piece of media with a transformative fandom, or the affirmative or transformative work in and of itself. It's a genre, a game, a creative storytelling mechanism, a strict rules-based play system, a maths-heavy piece of confusion, a fandom of its own making based on things other players will never know about because they are only in your game, or it's a multimillion dollar live-play show growing a fandom for everyone. And all the while we can all make memes about horny bards and big, himbo paladins.

There's even a whole genre of TikTok videos that are basically TTRPG come digital cosplay performances/LARPs that have generated not only their own content and stories based on the lore of TTRPGs but have from that created their own fanbases and inspired more folks to do the same in an ever growing spiral of fantasy game fan fun.

All of this, TTRPGS, nerdcore, cosplay, zines and fanworks of all types, goes to show that there is much more crossover at each point of fandom than people might think. You may not enjoy fic but you like a nerdcore track about your 'blorbo', you may not want to see canon appear changed in art but you love seeing cosplays at con, it all co-exists and, actually, it may well be worth engaging with things you may not have seen as your type of fandom engagement in the past. There is something to be said for there always being more at the table even if it's not your favourite thing to eat, just pass on the broccoli to the person who wants it and you get a big spoonful of the horseradish and it doesn't matter if a little edible tree gets on your plate, you might find your tastes change if you give it a try.

Above and below: Break out the D20s, we're going adventuring!

Above and overleaf pages: Tell your own stories and build your own fandom in the best way possible with imagination and miniatures.

TTRPG Live Play game *Dice of the Beholder's Chronicles of Nidum.*

Charity Live stream *Gender Quest* playing *Dungeons and Dragons* for 24 hours solid, featuring yours truly!

Cosplayers playing DnD, while dressed at the party from live play DnD game *Critical Role*, bit meta really. Photo by Megaera Amis.

TTRPGs are having such a renaissance there's even been a *Dungeons and Dragons* film this year! Image from MovieStills.com.

Not all tabletop games are the same: boardgame *Castles of Burgundy* is very different to DnD.

WHERE?

A Place of Our Own

Looking back on my own time as a fan, I can pinpoint the first time that I 'formalised' my admiration for something. I'll admit that I am not really a fanclub type of person, there is more ebb and flow to enjoy in my own experience and while I have my interests, each has its season. Some seasons are longer than others, but it is hard to tell in the moment what will last the test of time. That being said, I can clearly see my one and only fanclub acceptance pack to this day: the fanclub for Brian Jacques' *Redwall* books, and I was eight years old.

I shared this love with my best friend, looking at the recipes, merchandise, artwork and letters that came with the membership; we were a club of two amongst many.

We might not have been able to talk with the other people involved directly but it's the first time I remember thinking that there was more than just the little group of us who read these books at school, we were in the fanclub with the other fans, cool right? No, it was deeply uncool at the time, and probably still is, but I have held it as a very fond memory. And I still have some of the fanclub merchandise too.

Official fanclubs have, for the most part, taken a bit of a back seat as the fandom space of choice but they are still alive and kicking too for those who like something a bit more structured. You are more likely to see conventions, meets, social media and online chat rooms like Discord as the big players in fandom spaces these days but they still serve the same purpose.

The term fanclub does seem a little old fashioned now, something that your parents and grandparents might have done in their youth, or they are hanging on from a time before, but the space they provide for fans is as important as it's ever been. And while you might not think it, any fan community that is actively moderated, with rules and a set topic, kind of counts as a fanclub, no matter if it's official or not. A lot of the best clubs are ones no one gave you permission to have in the first place.

Having a place that is for fans to gather, talk and share has always been at the heart of fandom, and if it wasn't, what was all that in part one, eh? Fans need a place of their own – and there's the section title, got in early this time – to do all that cringey stuff that fans do, and I mean that very affectionately. As a creator it's hard to be in the mix with your fans for obvious reasons – either you are God and then you should worry about what happens when you mess up, or it's hard to see your work being touched and talked about in the 'wrong' way by others – so fans having places where creators should dare not tread is no bad thing, but more than that, it gives fans a place to work out how they want to be a fan and learn about the culture of fandom.

Throughout this book the term community has come up in one way or another, certainly there have been an awful lot of synonyms for it and sideways looks at the idea. It is, in its essence what this exploration into fan culture is about, community and the need for it in a very simple way, but community can't be built with nowhere to lay its foundations. You need to know where to go and what to look for, and that is something that fans have always been very good at creating.

Have You Tried Turning it Off and Online Again?

It's pretty hard to ignore the fact that much of modern fan spaces are in the online world. We see it every day on our social media, Discord servers, YouTube front page, even in the news from time to time; these online spaces have been for the last few decades the home of fandom and fan culture. Thinking back to the history of fandom, all the way back in part one, and the way that fandom has progressed it's not hard to see why it has spread its many legs out into all aspects of the web. It is the perfect space for it, but what does that actually mean and what are these spaces when you really look at them?

Most fan culture as we know it today comes from, to use an internet term, 'being chronically online' and I use that term with no small amount of tongue in cheek whilst also being aware that it is somewhat true that a lot of fans spend a lot of time online in order to connect with their community. And I don't think that's a bad thing – all things in moderation and all that, but still the point stands.

Just to recap part one, from all those thousands of words ago, fandom before the internet was reliant on you stumbling across other fans or learning that fan spaces, conventions, clubs and the like, existed so that you could engage with them. There are plenty of stories of folks who loved all these things, would dress up as characters, video their favourite shows, chat about them with friends at school, even write fanfic, but they did it almost in isolation. If a fan draws fanart in the woods and there's no one around to see it does it still count as fandom? That is something of the question. But once you have access to the internet? Well, hello whole world of fandom to jump into.

Early days of fandom online, it must be admitted, was sort of the Wild West. It wasn't all that easy to gain access to fandom unless you were on the right newsletters, could find the right forums, or had people to tell you where to go, and even then, you'd probably find the music stopped and every eye would turn on you the moment you stepped through the saloon doors into the fan space.

Pre-Google you were still very much at the whim of what you could muddle your way to, but fan servers soon became full of folks wanting to connect. And it's brilliant, right up to the early '00s, forums, LiveJournal and newsletters were still king, giving fans the space to flourish. Nothing is ever perfect, far from it, and fandom has never been far from fallings out, 'cancellings' and general drama, but it tended to be kept to a single fandom and no one else was any the wiser apart from through the grape vine. People could discuss their own ideas of fandom in the spaces they liked, in relative peace. Fandom has never been calm, but it was more, shall we say, contained.

But that all changed when social media attacked.

What? Did you think there wasn't going to be an *Avatar: The Last Airbender* reference in here?

Social media, particularly Twitter, Instagram and most recently, TikTok, have all but removed the lines of fandom spaces, with each fandom group and sub-group having their own little pocket to head off into where they are unlikely to be disturbed.

There's a change in online behaviour at this point. Fans are suddenly seeing people they didn't even know existed in their fandom saying that they are fans in a completely different way and with completely different ideas to what your group have decided are canon, fanon or headcanon. Shocking no one, this did lead to some interesting moments but that isn't what we are here to talk about. Yet. What it does do is give us, my intrepid explorers, a basis for understanding online spaces.

In the Land of Online

Have you ever heard the term 'Fandom TikTok' or 'Star Wars Twitter' or 'Science Side of Tumblr'? These, and a myriad of other versions of these terms, are used by online fans to describe the areas of their social media platform of choice that are dedicated to one fandom or fandom as a whole. These are basically the forums of today. The discussion spaces for people to talk about their fandom with other fans, post and get feedback on their fanworks, and generally see what is going on in the world of nerdom beyond their immediate environment.

They build up organically with people linking up with each other through searching hashtags, sharing, following and posting actively in with those tags, and also the sites showing you the 'you might like' options that they have now.

It doesn't take long for fans to find each other this way without ever needing to open a search engine.

It's been shown on TikTok that you can get the algorithms speed-running you into the heart of a fandom, or other topic, within four hours and that is no less true of Twitter or Instagram. Because of this it doesn't take long for you to feel included in these online spaces. You click into the way people work just by lurking around, and start to decode what's being talked about the longer you're there. It's a bit like *Clockwork Orange* were you start to figure out what on Earth is being said but in a slightly less terrifying and eye-opening way.

Online terminology has all but become its own form of language at this point. It's not just words or phrases, it's images, videos, gifs, sound clips, all acting as interconnected references that are so niche to internet culture, often specifically fan culture, that it is all but unintelligible to anyone looking in. The level of memes, shared knowledge and understanding gets so deep that it is almost code.

Each fandom is likely to have its own set of terms, including but not limited to ship names, terms for media titles or episode names, and describing fans of certain parts of the fandom, whilst also all using crossover terms and language that are universal to online fan spaces. It adds to a sense of belonging for your group and in the community as a whole. Back to our nerdy stacking dolls.

It's not just online that this happens, all fan-spaces do this, including the pre-internet ones. The Tolkien Society use 'Oxenmoot' as the name of their gathering, Discworld fans talk about 'Clatches', and Trekkies, well, that would be a whole book to itself going into that. But with the internet becoming more open and fan spaces having to mess around alongside each other with no real barriers, terms have blurred and joined and become more of a group language than they were before.

Tumblr is particularly well known for this, referring itself as a meme within the site as much as it references memes historically, never letting anything die. Do you know what the Misha-pocalypse was? Or the ball pit? Or spiders-Georg, because I do and I bet most people who were on Tumblr at any point in the last 15 years do too unless they were completely out of the loop – which given the fact that you can make yourself a little bubble on Tumblr, similar to old style forums, could happen.

For a long time in the '00s and '10s Tumblr was the go-to website for fans. It had both the 'open-world' vibe of Twitter and Instagram whilst also allowing you to completely curate your experience by following blogs, having a working block and mute system for tags and other users should you wish to do so, and by not showing you anything outside of what you had chosen to see. Algorithms were not going to be messing things up. That and the fact that the add-ons designed to improve it really did the work, made Tumblr a place where fans flocked. It still is, though in lesser numbers.

Something that Tumblr users did which mirrored the way that forums and newsletters worked was the use of blog separation. Rather than having all of your fandom posts on one blog, people would have a separate blog and username for each fandom they actively engaged in and created content for. Much like moving from forum to forum so as not to cross over your fandoms, separate blogs allowed for users to follow other accounts specialising in one thing on that account and others on another and you could switch between them with a mouse click instead of having to log out and in again.

This meant that fandoms were able to maintain a certain level of separate-ness because the fans wanted to do so. Of course, this wasn't for everyone, but multi-fandom blogs that chopped and changed had their own place as personal fan experiences that were more like a diary or journal of ideas than anything else. They could be compared to the commonplace books of the Victorian era that acted as places for thoughts, images, articles, or anything the person wanted to be collected and shared with other fans.

Talking again with Professor Matt Hills about this and what fandom spaces online looked like and will look like in the future:

> 'There's almost always been, you know, a platform that's been seen as kind of more fandom friendly. And whether it was sort of Live Journal or whether it moved to Tumblr, and then obviously, there was sort of mass migration kind of off Tumblr at certain point as well. But to a degree tends to kind of reshape or craft the fandom in particular ways. So, people have argued that Tumblr fandom enabled a much more fluid kind of multi fan kind of approach to fandom where it was much less about, you know, being in your fan object kind of silo.'

I'm about to show my age but I remember the days where folks on Tumblr were making 'Tumblr university' posts or 'Tumblr maps' to show how all the major fandom elements existed together and what tags to follow to get to different 'areas' of the site. I've actually seen this repeating on TikTok, so clearly the land of fandom never changes, but just gets a new access point.

This mix of single fandom areas and multi-fandom spaces that were curated by and for fans without the intervention of any outside influence was, and is, unique. It led to some of the most insane fandom moments of the 2010s, including a 'Tumblr convention' called DashCon that failed miserably, including not paying guests, hotels or the venue, and getting a reputation for being the Social Justice Warrior website due to the huge moments of discourse that happened between fans, but what it achieved in bringing fans together has yet to be replicated by any fan space since.

'[T]here are different kinds of platforms, pathways through fans, and different ways of doing fandom. Which may be generational up to a point. But yeah, if you're someone who kind of has grown up with Tumblr fandom, which was true for a lot of my students now, and then their sense of what it means to be a fan is, is quite specific,' Matt says, and from my own experience I can agree. The way that Tumblr shaped my fan experience and the experiences of the others I knew on the platform is very clear and has made an impact on how fandom is going forward.

TikTok is definitely trying to recreate this feeling as a fan space, though everyone on the app would probably deny that, and it's not quite managing it in the same way. The fact that Tumblr had a majority fanbase of nerdy people, primarily due to social media still finding its feet when it appeared on the scene in 2007, and then the aforementioned reputation it gained of being the weird website, meant it wasn't going to have the average person on the street using it; they were all on Twitter.

That being said, the curational element and the sectioned areas of fandoms have made their way onto TikTok, if not in quite the same way. The open-for-everyone nature of TikTok that means you could stumble across anything as you scroll once again blurs the edges of fandom content and groupings. You could be on *Star Wars* TikTok and someone with no connection to that at all could suddenly find themselves there and start to cause issues. Or they could suddenly find a brand new thing that they didn't know they would like. TikTok lacks boundaries, your curation is only as useful as the algorithm allows and it is definitely part of the way that fandom is moving forward, though not the only one by a long shot.

'If Tik Tok has become dominant [home for fandom],' Matt continues, 'then Discord is probably sort of emerging, or is sort of on the rise, I think at the moment really. And sometimes these things have relatively short kind of shelf lives. Other times, they really take hold, and you can have sort of a generation of fans whose fandom has been shaped by specific kind of platform experiences.'

Where TikTok is making open season for everyone to see everything, the other side of the coin is Discord. Discord is more akin to old school forums, with different groups with boards and moderators within them to give people space and safety to talk about what they love. However, unlike forums, unless you know how to get into a Discord group or you are invited, it might as well not exist. You're stuck on the outside.

These are private, often locked, spaces for groups of fans or friends to talk without being interrupted by others. The complete opposite of TikTok. You have the choice between open to all, or just a select few, and not much in the middle. Which is probably why Tumblr is still dragging along its half dead body of a server, keeping itself going despite everything. People want a middle ground and until something comes along to give fans that space again, Tumblr will continue to be it.

Let's Get Physical

Here we see the fan, in their natural habitat, sharing niche memes and posting takes on their favs to the internet while standing in a circle at a convention in various states of cosplay or nerdy clothing. Once they are feeling recharged from each other's memes and have posted a TikTok of the event, they will move off back into the crowds in order to buy merchandise and browse the art of fellow fans.

That is what I did for a weekend four or five times a year in my teens, though we were all on a DS or a PSP rather than mobile phones because I am old and social media apps weren't quite there yet. It was great. Conventions are still great and it's heartening to see teenagers doing exactly what I did when I first came into fandom spaces like this, and interacting with the wider fan-sphere through the online spaces at the same time.

I spent a lot of my teens meeting at a local library manga and anime club for teenagers. It was one of the places I got my first buzz for all of this outside of just talking with mates, or hanging around in online spaces, and it was here that I learnt that I could *go* to conventions. They were a real thing, in the place that I lived; they weren't just a thing in big city America like I saw on TV. Now, when I tell you I was so excited at my first convention that I literally don't remember parts of it, I'm not lying. There are photos from the day that I have no memory of taking, and even over a decade later I still can't recall some of it, no matter how hard I try.

While a lot of fandom goes on in online spaces in the modern age, and often in letter writing in the past, this does not mean that there aren't physical fan spaces and that they remain a hugely important part of fan culture for all of us. Meeting up with your fandom friends, be that at an event for a certain fandom or a border space where multiple fandoms crossover, has always been a part of the fan experience and has only gotten more popular in the form of large scale events. Having places to share the discussion is a long running tradition of fan-culture; we are but the nerdy descendants of nerdy ancestors.

There's something about getting to be nerdy in a space designed for you to do that, physically there with your mates and tens, hundreds, thousands, maybe tens of thousands of other fans that just hits different.

It isn't just conventions either. Like I said, I went to an anime club that only had 15 of us in it, and that was just as formative and important as the massive cons were. There are board game cafes, comic book shops with reading areas and coffee machines, video game drop-ins, local clubs in libraries, book groups, meet-ups, smaller local conventions even; look around and suddenly you'll see fan culture everywhere and fans wanting to hang out in one way or another.

These spaces are built by fans, for fans. Community hubs that don't have the price tag that comes with attending multiple conventions a year, nor do they have the same crowds and overwhelming atmosphere that even the most hardened convention goer can struggle with. They are often set up with the idea of being more than places that existing groups of friends can hang out in too, having open events for anyone to come along and meet new people, try out new things or learn a new skill. Many of them run crafting groups for miniature figure painting, cosplay making, comic book drawing or even nerdy knitting groups. Whatever your brand of nerdiness, spaces like this are going have something for you because they are made by people like you.

Companies, arts groups and educational institutions have all seen the benefit of tapping into fandom by opening up more physical spaces in one way or another. One of the joys of fan culture being seen as something more important than maybe it has in the past century, is that it isn't just the fans themselves organising things anymore. Now it's museums, libraries, book launches, film launches, TV show launches; all the launches that have all got in on the fan action. You'll have cosplayers at NASA next at this rate, get it? Launches? NASA. Yeah, it's bad but please can we have cosplayers at NASA, it would be so cool. The cast of *Star Trek* got to, so why not the fans, eh?

Libraries and schools up and down the UK have begun bringing in clubs, events and speakers focused on pop culture to create spaces for fans to come together. Talks and events have always been a thing in fandom, since the get go of anything you could call fandom. You have the salons and coffee house meetings, discussing with authors and poets about their work: the tours of authors like Dickens to sold-out playhouses, signings, comic book store parties, fan-organised discussion evenings, and much more. While some of that has morphed into the conventions and fan clubs of the modern day, some have stayed just as they always were, if not with a little bit more of a twenty-first century twist.

Both the British Museum and the Science Museum in London have invited fans along to exhibition openings for video games and manga in recent years, wanting to both encourage other fans to come and to celebrate the exhibitions themselves through their fans. The fact that such prestigious museums are having these exhibitions at all, let alone inviting the fans along, shows how much these institutions are starting to value the input of the community. The British Museum has even hosted cosplay catwalk shows, guest lecturers on pop culture and the premiere of Marvel's *Moon Knight* TV show.

It's hardly uncommon for a fanclub to be invited along to fill up the first row at a gig or be in the audience for an interview. Managers and marketing executives know how to get the best optics and having the people who love your rock star/band/actor/writer/piece of media the most are going to make for a great shot to send to the press. And the fans get a great experience out of it too.

Shocking no one, Disney have gotten in on this with fan events being run around the premieres and launches for pretty much everything to do with the Marvel and *Star Wars* franchises. They are clever cookies there at Disney.

Back in 2022, while in the midst of researching I was invited to attend one of these fan events: the *Thor: Love and Thunder* premiere. The fans in question were cosplayers, an instant draw for the crowd and a great photo op for the stars of the film. Despite having been to many fan events, conventions and meet-ups in my time, there was something palpably different about this. The nervous electricity in the air the group waited in, what I can only describe as a 'fan pen', on the red carpet. Some back and forth with the photographers grabbing snaps before the big names arrived to find out who exactly was coming and when; it was nerve-racking to say the least.

And then the stars were there. The favourite actors, directors, the characters that these fans loved, grabbing pictures, snapping a selfie or two and then gone.

It lasted maybe two minutes before each celeb was whisked away. A blink and you miss it moment, but a moment that was so special to each one of those fans.

As the fly on the wall of all this, and yet still a fan myself, I couldn't help feeling all this too. I'll hold my hands up to momentarily forgetting how to talk when Taika Waititi showed up, but I also couldn't help but feel small amount of the staging of it all. But, hey, it's a film premiere, that was always going to happen.

With companies including fandom as part of their media or marketing, there's a balance between fans being used for press and fans being celebrated at these events as part of what supports these pieces of media. You can meet the fans where they want to be met and invite them into the spaces that have been made for them by companies, but sometimes said companies try a little to hard to be 'down with the kids'. It's a tough line to walk and one that is becoming harder to walk every day.

Above, below and opposite: The British Museum's *Citi Exhibition: Manga* bringing manga and anime to mainstream culture. Photos by Megaera Amis.

Left: Cosplayers helping the manga jump off the page at The British Museum. Photo By Megaera Amis.

Below and opposite: Nothing like the buzz of being at a convention with all the other fans! Photos by Alasdair Watson.

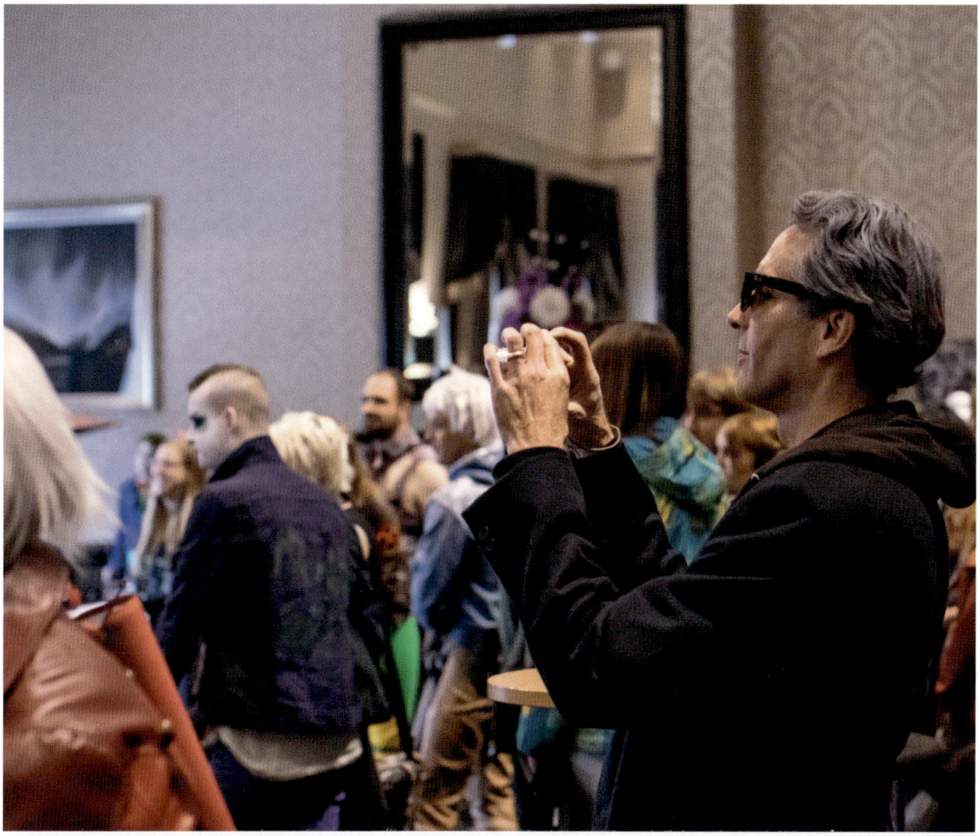

Cosplay Comes to Europe
ACME COMIC CON
ACME COMIC CON

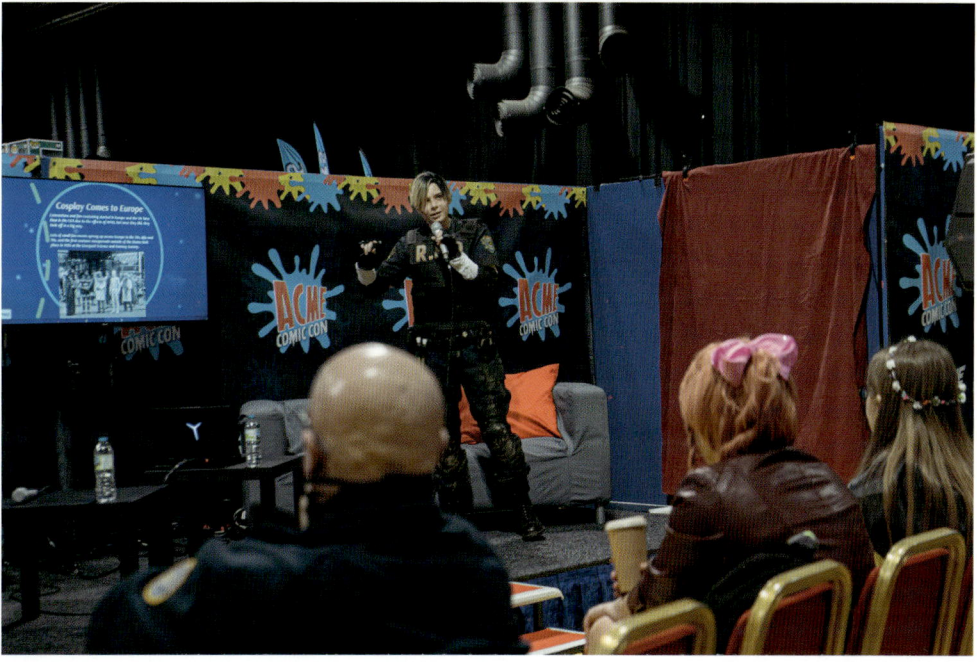

Above and below: London MCM Comic Con is always a big draw for fans. Photos by big-ashb, Creative Commons BY 2.0.

Above: San Diego Comic Con, the worlds biggest convention, nerd heaven! Photo by Gage Skidmore, Creative Commons BY-SA 2.0.

Below: *The Lord of the Rings* in concert. Seeing the movie with a live orchestra is a big draw for fans. Photo by Tony Peters, Creative Commons BY 2.0.

Above: E-Sports, you think you've seen fandom? There's nothing quite like getting in a stadium to watch your favourite video games. Photo by Jakob Wells, Creative Commons BY 2.0.

Below: You can even see video games in museums now!

Space Invaders

There is this misconception of fans that they are mindless consumers. If you are fan of something you will want to buy, consume and generally absorb every little thing about your fandom that is thrown at you. This is not true.

Fans are not dancing monkeys jumping to the will of the corporations pumping out endless streams of media. We pick and choose what we like, what we don't, and when needed we make it known through our money that something isn't working for us – or in strange petitions about removing films from canon because it didn't match up perfectly with the fanfic in our heads. It may not even be the whole fanbase having opinions about something, often it's not, but fans on the whole will not simply eat up everything they are given.

'If fandom was formed alongside and through and within the rise of consumer culture, it did also contest that,' Professor Matt Hills says. '[L]ook at the classic beginning of fan studies work, Henry Jenkins' *Textual Poachers*, it's about fandom as kind of being anti-commercial. Fandom didn't want to sell out.'

Fandoms as a rule tend to run organically, through new media that is provided, yes, but more importantly through a large amount of those fanworks we talked about. If a piece of media doesn't have fanworks, or if fanworks stop being credited within a few weeks of the thing coming out, it likely isn't going to stay the course growing any sort of fandom. Fans know this, they can feel it in the water, feel it in the air, when the world is changing with a new fandom coming into being around something. They know the behaviours, so they also know when something just isn't going to work. It can be disappointing if you liked the thing but if it's not happening, it's not happening.

This brings me to the subject of *Goncharov* (Martin Scorsese, 1973).

Goncharov, a lost film by Martin Scorsese, was rediscovered in 2022 by Tumblr users who then proceeded to bring the film back to the mainstream through analysis, fanworks and general fandom behaviour. The internet was overjoyed. No one had ever seen such a flood of art, fancams, fics, and meta appear in such a short amount of time, especially not for a cult gangster film of the 1970s. It was unprecedented.

Except, it never existed.

The entire thing was fake, made-up based on a picture of a knock off designer boot with the made-up film on the label. From this one image came a spiralling mass of content, from people creating the plot of the movie and linking it all together with users they had never met, to a full score being made again by multiple people with no idea that anyone else was doing this, to 'iconic' lines and homoerotic tension of every variety. By the end of the day a whole fandom and all its hallmarks, had appeared online.

If you look on Ao3 there are even more fanfics than some actual films, including James Cameron's *Avatar* (at time of writing). The people making this fandom had a deep and intimate knowledge of how fandom works, its trappings, and how to make one for themselves out of literally nothing, for the fun of it. They did it more successfully than any purpose-built marketing plan ever could because they understood the ins and outs of what would fuel a fandom to grow and that by taking it seriously in this way other fans would want to be in on the joke too. That they would want to make fun of themselves whilst also celebrating the weirdness of fannish behaviour.

For a few wonderful weeks you could feel the collective amusement of 'aren't we very silly doing our silly little things but, oh what silly joy it brings us' flowing out of Tumblr – where else did you think this happened? – and the rest of the internet as this niche and deep-rooted piece of jokey, meta commentary of fan culture made its way around.

It's not the first time this has been attempted, though this is possibly one of the few times it hasn't been an organised or at least thought through idea. TikTok users decided, during the COVID lockdown, to make a fake '80s/'90s TV show about pirates, and it worked pretty well. When I was at university, a few friends and I maintained that a fake anime existed for weeks and other people just hadn't seen it because it was only on VHS.

The thing with *Goncharov*, is how far it went as both an idea and within the understanding of the fans of how fandom works. It was meta within meta within meta, spiralling up and out of the control of the original joke and into something that reflected what fans know about themselves, that it doesn't happen without them. And you can't force feed them content either, the joy of being a fan has to go hand in hand with the media that they are engaging with and a lot of that joy is homemade. You can't buy that sort of interaction, but that doesn't stop people from trying.

Fandom by Numbers

Algorithmic fandom, can it be done? Short answer? No, not really. Not in any sort of long run, sustainable way. Long answer?

In the last few years we've seen more and more attempts to create 'fan' style content from the big players of media. It could be the quirky games on the YouTube channels of magazines and media news sites, getting the stars of movies to make TikToks to seem natural and relatable all the while having their personal social media tightly controlled by themselves or an agent, Reddit Q&As, the list goes on. All of this is just the press tour now for any given piece of media that comes out, and it is all in fan spaces to a greater or lesser extent.

Author note: This is obviously for a myriad of reasons and is in no way a bad thing for 'celebs' to do this, not least for their own mental health, but it is interesting to see how reality and fandom space is controlled and/or managed in this way in aid of marketing.

Many of these things have the feel of the fanworks that fans are already making. The YouTube videos and TikToks are akin to the fancams and clips that people make from interviews on the red carpet, on the news, blooper reels or similar, but premade. The Q&As feel like they are leaning into what fans want, rather than being a piece in a newspaper or magazine that is more obviously a professional piece, the ones on Reddit and Tumblr, even YouTube, are masquerading, to some extent, as a legitimate, personal meeting with fans while just being as controlled as ever.

Is this strictly a bad thing? Probably not. Is it a bit like having your parents show up to a party and crash your style? Yes, just a bit. With the added thing of 'give us money for the content' layered into every inch of it. This style of marketing does get people engaged in the new thing, but, as with a lot of marketing, it lacks staying power. You have to keep reminding people to come back with more and more marketing content to keep it going; it fails at the first fandom hurdle, which is to get fans to be creative in their own way.

What they are trying to do is to generate a fandom presence around something by doing some of the work for fans for them without realising that doing that work is part of the fun. This is why it doesn't generate new fandom. Half the joy of making fanworks is the weird and wonderful ideas that people come up with to feed the beast. Strange little comments that end up as in-jokes within a micro-fandom, or memes that make no sense unless you have a decade's worth of knowledge for that – may I direct you to the icecream maker man in *Star*

Wars: The Empire Strikes Back – or 'crack' ships and art that makes the whole fandom go 'OH NO'.

Mostly these marketing techniques are going to be picked up on by those who are already invested in an actor or a franchise but don't tend to engage new people or create a new fandom for that thing on its own, so if you have something completely new, this type of fandom focus marketing just doesn't work. I mean, look at the *Fast and the Furious* 'family' meme explosion. It was everywhere for a few weeks around the newest film coming out, but does anyone really even remember it beyond being a slightly odd marketing choice?

Fandom survives and thrives through people wanting to engage with it. Either this is through the thing itself being so popular that it lasts in the 'dark ages' without new content coming out, or never having any new content, purely due the hardcore fans who love it. This is the case for so many of the major fandoms: *Lord of the Rings, Star Wars, Star Trek* and *Doctor Who* have all had decades long breaks between new additions to their respective franchises. Or you have fandoms that seem to build themselves out of all but the dregs of a single piece of content, but we will get to that later. The other option is that you, as a media company, keep throwing shiny, 'fun', new stuff at people to make sure they are constantly interested in what is happening next – hello *Marvel Cinematic Universe* (MCU).

Ah yes. Let's talk about the *MCU*.

It is one of the greatest media success stories around, with a huge fanbase, ranging all over the fandom swimming pool. It's done what nerds over the world had only dreamt of, made superheroes super mainstream. It is, in no small part, a key element of the whole geek-chic thing and has becoming a staple of pop culture in and outside fandom spaces. Well done, Marvel.

Or should that be well done, Disney? And that's the thing. The *MCU*, with the backing of Disney, blew up, once it had past the tests of popularity and proved itself beyond that first *Iron Man* movie. When Disney bought Marvel and all the properties that went with that – and slowly picked up all the other characters that Marvel had sold off to the likes of Fox and Sony in the early '00s – really collecting them like *Pokémon* cards aren't they? – they got a product that had a brand new fanbase who had found these characters through the movies, and an old fanbase that has been starved of big blockbuster content. What a golden egg they have.

The *MCU* took advantage of this by making as much content as they could, building up to the point where multiple films and TV shows were coming out a year. In 2022 alone, nine new Marvel projects made it onto the big and small screen, all but one of which crossed over with previous projects in someway and were required viewing for future content to make sense. You have to watch it all to find out what's going on and that can cause one of two things to happen. One: fans watch everything, buy everything, and the new content keeps them hooked, or two: they get burnout both in their wallet and in their brain.

If you are causing your fanbase to burn out by pushing too much content on them, it doesn't matter how good that content is – Marvel really do have a formula that works, there are good, fun films on the whole – they stop engaging. They find something else.

The push to create as much content as possible to grow and build up fandoms in order to keep profit up can actually have a very negative effect on a core part of your audience. You need water to live, but too much and you drown.

I am a big fan of comics, have been since I was a kid, and I see the way that comic books, particularly the American style comics, are reflected in the movies. Big crossover events, characters from different stories having a team-up, massive world building, all of these are staples of the genre of superhero comics. It's part of what makes comics work. But it doesn't work so well for movies.

Serialised comics are basically like soap operas. They are ongoing stories that have run over decades, with over-the-top characters and ridiculous changes in narrative in order to keep the fun going. You can dip in and out and it doesn't matter all that much because they acknoweldge that there is so much history you are unlikely to know, or need to know, it all. If you are picking up a comic once a week, once a month, or even getting the collected versions of the stories, you are getting your little hit of the next segment of the story and then you wait for the next chapter.

With a movie you don't want it to be a chapter, you want it to be the whole story. You also don't want to go to the sequel a year later and not have a clue what is happening because you didn't watch two other films and a TV show. Fans start to burnout and they disengage.

The *MCU* is by no means the only example of this, plenty of franchises push for fans to engage with them constantly in this sort of way, but it is the biggest and most obvious. You can see it with videogames like *Overwatch* and *Fortnight* having new drops of items or DLCs or character skins all the time too. Constantly pumping new and shiny things into the fans' heads to get them to stay engaged and pay for the content.

But as I said before, fans are not just dancing monkeys and for all the love in the world, trying to force fandom by numbers, be it by ads, by constant content creation, or by coming into their space, it will never be the same as the way fandoms create themselves.

Plant the Seed and See What Grows

Let's go back to *Goncharov*. The reason I started this little sub-chapter with that is because it illustrates so well what anyone trying to generate fandom fails to understand: you can't predict it. You just can't. You can try, put out something that ought to tick every fandom happy box under the sun and get nothing, all the while some random piece of media, with no marketing, promotional work or anything can pop up on the internet out of nowhere and suddenly have more fanworks than you can shake a stick at.

Goncharov is not real. Yet I know that Katya and Sofia have sapphic, shipping energy for the whole movie and that the clocks throughout the movie symbolise the movement towards the inescapable end for these characters. Why do I know that? Because the fanart, the essays, the music videos, were all so engaging that it spiked my curiosity well before I knew it was a joke, and the joke just made it all better. People saw it being shared and wanted to find out what this strange fandom that sprung out of the ether was.

Fandom works by word of mouth, or should I say word of reblog? Maybe retweet depending on your platform of choice. Fans are more than a little vocal about what it is they like. They post it everywhere, and all the ads in the world won't get you the same interest as a beautiful piece of heartfelt fanart, or a gif set illustrating the tragic fall from grace of someone's fav. You can't know what is going to tickle the fancy of enough people for them to get the word spread. Though, you could always give gay pirates a try, that seems to do pretty well.

It was while I was researching this book that *Our Flag Means Death* made its rather underwhelming first step onto the fandom scene. I was sent a message by a friend who worked at HBO that I should check out this new show. 'You're a nerd who likes historical stuff, Taika Waititi and *Flight of the Concords*, you'll love this. Trust me.'

I am massively paraphrasing, if in fact he ever said it like that at all, but the recommendation was made.

I watched the first four episodes. They were coming out two a week, and about to hit the third week of airing, and since I was a little behind, and definitely not procrastinating, I gave it a watch thinking it would pass the time. Which it did, pleasantly enough for the first couple of episodes. A brief look online told me that not many people were talking about it and there was little marketing for the show. This coupled with the issue of it being on a streaming service that wasn't super available meant that it wasn't really hitting a big audience. But I enjoyed it. It fitted in well with my work schedule so when the next two aired I put them on in my break and everything changed.

The show went from silly, historical comedy to queer romcom in the blink of an eye and suddenly I wasn't the only person I knew watching it. It was everywhere. Not trending, no not yet, but word was spreading. People were passing on the show, they were sharing and posting and it was word of mouth to word of mouth to word of mouth and then everyone wanted to watch it.

Was it really a queer pirate romcom about Blackbeard? Were there really queer characters in a period comedy? Trans characters? Openly gay? And not playing it for laughs? Well not those laughs. The gun powder was lit my friends, and golly it was not going to be snuffed out. Literally overnight fanart, fanfic, discussions, meta, Twitter threads, Tumblr gifsets, all came out of nowhere. It blew up. And what I wouldn't give to know how many marketing execs wish they could get that sort of press for their show. Author Note: I am very aware that the second season has been widely advertised in a way that has more than made up for the lack of for season one. It's amazing to see a show like this, that is such a champion of diversity and humanity be celebrated in the form of giant billboards and Superbowl spots. OFMD fandom, I salute you.

It is important that I say that this show, if you haven't yet heard about it, is a queer romcom about a load of outsiders, many of whom are people of colour, who are all given time to be both funny and taken seriously for who they are. The reason this is important is because, if you hadn't guessed it by now, a lot of fandom people are outsiders who aren't often given that time and space in the real world and many of them are queer and people of colour. If you didn't get that from the fanfic chapter then I don't know what to tell you.

Fandoms like this grow because they are what people want, they are what people are crying out for. *Our Flag Means Death* was this perfect tonic to the big, brash, box office media by numbers. It told a story that people desperately wanted to see because it was the first time that the story was about them in some way and that meant that it tapped into the way that fan culture works in a way that meant a fandom grew around it so passionately that they, after one season of the show being on air, were writing letters, emails, making blogs and begging for season two to be made. Just like *Star Trek* fans seeing a diverse cast on TV for the first time and pulling together to get the show going. Just like *Sherlock Holmes* fans wanting to be part of the story, needing to know what happened next and dragging Holmes back from the dead. *Our Flag Means Death* is the next in a long history of self-made fandoms holding up their show and keeping it together with fanfic, art and hope.

Above, below, opposite and overleaf: Fans at the *Thor: Love and Thunder* premiere in London, meeting star Natalie Portman and director Taika Waititi. (Photography by Megaera Amis)

Megaera Amis
MEGGOPHOTO

Megaera Amis
MEGGOPHOTO

Right: The original *Goncharov* shoe and the beginnings of the meme, from Reddit.

zootycoon-archive   Follow
Aug 21, 2020

'THE GREATEST MAFIA MOVIE EVER MADE'
MARTIN SCORSESE PRESENTS
GONCHAROV
∙DOMENICO PROCACCIPRODUCTION
∙A FILM BY MATTED JWH J0715
ABOUT THE NAPLES MAFIA

i got these knockoff boots online and instead of the brand name on the tag they have the name of an apparently nonexistent martin scorsese movie??? what the fuck

loseremo   Follow
Aug 22, 2020

this idiot hasn't seen goncharov

abandonedambition

I HAVE AN ARMY

WE HAVE A FAMILY

Above, below left and below right: No meme is as strong as… family. Or *The Fast and the Furious* franchise.

Dom, what are you doing here?

You don't do that to family.

I am inevitable.

No… Family is inevitable

Above and below: Actor Kit Connor and the cast of *Heartstopper* on Netflix.

Above and overleaf: Writer for StarWars.com Bria LaVorgna cosplaying as Dr Aphra and a TIE fighter pilot from *Star Wars*.

As Above, So Below

Fandom is more than meets the eye. You never know if the fandom rolling on past you is actually just the little yellow beetle it looks like or if it's actually about to jump into your path fully robot-ed up in the middle of your social media feed. That is to say, there are plenty of fandoms that you have no idea what they are actually like, how deep they go, and how many odd and unusual, but successful, fandoms there are.

There is a veritable cornucopia of fandoms growing in their own sweet way in their own sweet time that people may have no idea they are even doing anything. Most of the time fandoms and their spaces are simply ships in the night to those outside of them and who might barely get a glance at what's inside to see the craziness within.

This really isn't unusual: it would be weird if you knew everything about every fandom knocking around in fan-land, and can often be a good thing, particularly if that fandom space is within a larger fandom. *The Clone Wars* fandom is a perfect example, having its own little fandom within the larger *Star Wars* fandom, with *The Bad Batch* having its own fandom within *The Clone Wars*. This allows for a space for fans who might struggle with the larger group space, but you might not even know that these smaller groups exist and just see *Star Wars* as a whole.

There are plenty of small fandoms that thrive without existing within a larger one too, and maybe have only a hundred or so people engaging with them, all managing to find each other – hi *A.J. Raffles* fandom; keep up the good work, Crime and Cricket brigade – but neither of these types of 'invisible' fandoms are the ones that get quite so mind boggling when you start to look deeper. Oh no, we're about to go for a deep dive.

Strap into James Cameron's deep-sea submarine because we're about to go hunting for the creatures that lurk in the sunless oceans of fandom, the weird ecosystems that you'd have no idea were there from the surface and the strange tentacle blobs that are so much bigger than they should ever have been. There are creatures out there that are just waiting to be woken from the depths and are so much more than you could ever know.

An Under Tale

I guarantee you, if you say the name *Undertale* to anyone outside of the fan sphere, they will have almost no idea what you are talking about. And yet it is possibly one of the most popular game series of the last two decades, with a fandom to match.

To breakdown what *Undertale* is, it is a short game made by Toby Fox and released in 2015, with a MASSIVE fandom work growing the multi-versal lexicon of the games canon to extremes that very few other fandoms have ever seen. There is also *Deltarune* that may or may not be a follow up, also made by Fox, that was initially released in 2018 as a chapter-based game with chapters one and two currently available.

Undertale allows the player to replay the game through multiple story paths (good, bad, morally unforgivable type thing) to give you a different experience each time. This is not that unusual in videogames. Except, in *Undertale* the game knows that you are doing this and the more you play, the more you change things, the more the game, and certain characters in the game, know what you are doing, and they know that you have taken certain endings or situations away.

You can get the good ending, replay to get the bad ending and get a worse one because you took the good ending away. It's a massive moral question about how you should approach these situations, and questions the player on their choices. It also means that the game in and of itself is a multiverse, and that is where, for us at least, it gets interesting.

When you have a game that by its very nature is an ever-expanding multiverse of stories that you are influencing, and there are characters within that setting that are reacting to you knowingly doing this, wouldn't you want to see how far you could push it?

And that is just what this fandom did. They took the idea of the fandom multiverse – that all these different stories and AUs can happen within fandom – and applied it to the canon because the canon itself was already doing that. Suddenly you have AU upon AU upon AU appearing and they start crossing over with each other, with the game, with the characters who are 'aware' of these multiverses being written, drawn and played with as if they knew all this was happening.

The works span every type of fanwork you can think of and more. People have animated the battle sequences from the game, they have made orchestral versions of the soundtrack – one version of the soundtrack ended up being used by the Pope during a presentation without knowing it was from this game – made their own ongoing cartoon shows on YouTube, made cosplays of AUs, all sorts of things. If you can think of it, there's an *Undertale* fan who's done it.

The thing is, it's all frustratingly good. We're talking top-tier animations with millions of views, endless web-comics, novel-length fanfics, the most intriguing and beautiful art you have ever seen retweeted all over the place and it's all come out of a five-hour 8-bit game! You'd be tricked into believing it was some great, magnum opus by some of these works. Not to say the game isn't good, it is very good, but the fanworks have spiralled out into a different class of fandom that you just wouldn't expect was there from the surface.

There are over a hundred documented AU unique versions of *Undertale* at this point – according to Fandomness_X3 on Wattpad, it's a pretty concise list.

This still might not sound that different from other fandoms, there are AUs and cool fanworks in all of them, but with *Undertale* what feels different is how these AUs aren't all your standard fandom AUs. Many are specific to *Undertale* due to the nature of the game, and how they have become so widely spread that it has led to people joining the fandom without ever playing the game and possibly only being a fan of a single AU version or the collective AUs as the story rather than the original game itself.

The *Undertale* fandom was, and is, sort of its own Disney. It is adding new and exciting ideas to the big pile of shiny content in an ever-trickling stream, but it's not a new blockbuster movie, or toy line being brought out by the company of origin, it's the fandom.

That is where this fandom sits in a class of its own. The interaction of the fandom with the original media is now so varied and broad that you can't help but see the fandom itself as the piece of the media. People are fans of *Undertale* as created by the fandom meaning that the game, now games, have stopped being the driving force of what the fans want. It is so self-perpetuating that even without *Deltarune* coming out, the fandom never needed Toby Fox to feed them new content ever again. As it was, *Deltarune* gave the fandom a burst of new energy on top of all of this, adding to the already endless mountain of content that the fandom had brought out itself.

It's no surprise that people become fans of these worlds without knowing what the original is. It would be hard not to be excited or impressed by the works that are being created just for the sheer love of it.

This fandom is huge, sprawling across fandom consciousness, but you leave the internet and it might as well not exist. It seems impossible that it can have such an impact on so many people and not leave an obvious mark outside of the digital world. It is so often the case for fandoms. You would never know they were there unless you start looking for them, because I'm certain *Undertale* isn't the only fandom like this out there, the others just may not have crossed my path yet, and yes, I know about *Homestuck*. I just told you I was on Tumblr.

Fandoms like this swim in the depths of the fandom ocean, they are beyond the deep end of the pool and into those places that light cannot pierce, but what about the ones so big that you don't even realise what you're walking around on top of isn't an island at all, until it moves.

The Turtle Moves

We think of large-scale fandoms as being these huge goliaths astride fan culture, the ones that appear in every toy shop, gadget store and internet meme page with titles like 'Eleven facts you didn't know about *Star Trek*' and then proceed to list eleven things you definitely did know. These are the ones that take up cultural space in a way that you just can't help but see. Except not always. Sometimes it's a bit less in your face than the 800th piece of Baby Yoda merch on the shelf and a little more like a sleeping kaiju waiting to lift its head.

These are the fandoms that are in the bones of the internet, the ones that live in the code, and have lived in the social consciousness without most knowing since before even that. Fandoms like *Discworld*.

I, like much of the population of the UK, am a massive fan of Sir Terry Pratchett and the *Discworld* books. They are some of the best examples of modern fantasy, managing to be both hilarious and an incredibly poignant look into the human condition. Plus, they have a man in a golden suit in them and I'm a sucker for a good cosplay idea. Thing is, I had no idea there was a fandom for *Discworld*. I knew people liked it, everyone I know has read Pratchett. I was given my first *Discworld* book aged twelve by a school librarian who knew I liked Tolkien and then a decade later I stood in a sweet shop in Bath with my best friend crying our eyes out the day Sir Terry passed away. I would call myself a fan, so how come I – and a hell of a lot of other people it turns out – didn't know there was a fandom?

Somehow this massive, and I mean massive, group of fans have hidden themselves in fabric of fan culture. They are everywhere. You mention *Discworld* around a group of nerds and they will come crawling out of every nook and cranny to talk about it. There is literal coding in the make up of websites with Terry Pratchett's name in it as a memorial to him. A hidden bumblebee tattoo or a spring of lilac in amongst the TARDIS and an X-wing, a donation to orangutan sanctuaries, or a gift of a tiny turtle charm at a convention. All of these are tiny, hidden acts of fandom that if you know, you know, but otherwise, you'd be none the wiser.

These types of fandoms are few and far between, or at least it seems as though they are.

The very nature of fandoms like this mean you just don't know about them until something raises the fans like sleeper agents being told 'it's unseasonably cold for July in Coventry' or some such – sure, I could have made an *MCU* reference here, but I'm not going to, they have had far too much of this chapter dedicated to them already – then these fans spill out of the woodwork like rats on a sinking ship but they love that ship and very much want you to know why those characters should be kissing, thank you very much.

The *Discworld* fandom I feel is one of the best examples of this and stands very much at the opposite end of the spectrum to a fandom like *Undertale* in its make up and conception for a myriad of reasons, the biggest and obvious of which being that several books in the series pre-date the internet. This still leads it to ending up being in a similar, somewhat underground place in the current fan ecosystem. Because the thing is, I don't think you'd know you were in the presence of *Discworld* fans, and other fandoms like them, until it is much too late to get out.

Like I said, it's not like they're quiet about it though. Everyone and their mum is a fan of Terry Pratchett. Okay, well not my mum but lots of other mums. You start talking about the books or share a piece of art or anything in fact *Discworld* related on any social media and you'll find that people you didn't even know liked these books, LOVE these books, and will go on about them for hours. And not just in a 'Oh yeah, I like those' way, but in a fandom way. They may not be doing the fandom thing, but you open your mouth about Pratchett, and everyone wants to dive right in.

This fandom is very definitely fannish, in an its own old school kind of way, but once you know what you're looking for you can't stop seeing this fandom, like you've broken out of the Matrix. It's part of the charm of the books that's reflected in the fandom; they are so full of hidden jokes, references, facts about the world, that it would make sense that, that would be mirrored in the way the fans talk about them. It's only once you've had your rabbit hole moment that you see it all.

A whole world of book groups, meme pages, meet-ups, Discord groups, discussion-led TikToks and newsletters opens up, like finding the way into L Space.

Author note: L Space; Library Space that is seemingly endless, a bit like a bag of holding but with books and an orangutan librarian.

Much like other older fandoms they have their own language and codes, with traditions built up over the years that would make zero sense to anyone from any other fandom, and even less to those outside of fandom entirely. This all means that they aren't super likely to show up as part of the more general fan culture spaces, like Comic Con, in a big way. Why would fans like this need to? Because they have their own conventions, and that was where the real fandom action was happening.

It was whilst I was researching for this book that I managed to get myself to The International Discworld Convention. I had, in actuality, been planning to go in 2020, as it runs on a two year cycle, but we all know what happened in 2020 and the whole event got pushed forwards to 2022. Not the end of the world and I definitely used that time well, finishing all my costumes for the International Maskerade (correct spelling) costume competition, and didn't have to con crunch in the month leading up to the event at all. But that is not the point.

I have been to a lot of conventions, events, meets, hangouts, etc in my time. I've been doing this since I was 15 after all, and I can say hand on heart, I have never been around fans like this. *Discworld* Con was literally another world.

Single fandom cons are a bit of a Universe of their own. You're not sharing space, you're just there with your people, your tribe, your fandom and you don't have to hunt down or fight for your special thing to have space. At Comic Con everyone is in together, it's amazing sure, but there is nothing quite like being in the midst of a crowd who are all there for the one thing.

At *Discworld* Con this comes in the form a group of people who span the length, breadth and depth of fandom experiences; range from those who have been fans since the beginning to those who have only just found their way here; people who sat at the bar and drank with the man himself, those who missed that boat but are still as dedicated as any other and everything in between. It's a special place to be.

What *Discworld* fandom feels like is a microcosm of all of fandom in one place. You can go back to those moments in history when a creator sat with their friends and fans and discussed their own works – that happened here. Early literary style fan clubs – that happened here. 'Zines, here. Letter writing, here. Costumes, here. Forums and online space building, here. Memes, here. It's all here, each moment in fandom in history is played out in miniature. It covers everything, possibly because its roots go so far out into the world whilst remaining almost untouched by the ways of large scale media.

It's a bit like a fungus, everywhere, all at once, but all that can be seen as a circle of mushrooms in the garden every now and then. And much the same as a circle of mushrooms, you should probably be aware of what might happen if you cross through the ring. You never know what you might get yourself into.

4 Creator and Fan: Finding the Balance

Fans and creators. Creators and fans. It's an interesting relationship. You rely on each other symbiotically, one can't exist unless the other is there. Creators feed the fandom and in return the fandom feeds the creator in a big, old circle of love and creativity. Harmony.

Unless the balance gets tipped and someone moves into the space they aren't meant to be. This harmonious existence can only last if people play the game by the rules, well, the guidelines. You can't suddenly go into a creator's space and demand that they give you what you want or suffer the consequences, nor can a creator dictate how they want their fans to be fans. That breaks the flow, and everything stops.

This once again brings us back to the role that online spaces play in fandom and the fact that everyone is essentially forced to play in the same playground most of the time. It comes up over and over, but the lack of spaces for fandom discourse, discussion and general silliness to take place, and the fact that people are encouraged by the online platforms to post more and more means that the boundaries are blurring at a rate of knots. And that's on both sides of the coin. Both fans and creators are struggling to know how to behave with each other when the world is open to everyone.

Online spaces have brought up an awful lot of questions for how fandom spaces and the way the culture of the fans in them has evolved. Can fans and creators co-exist in spaces like this or do there need to be firmer lines drawn for the peace of mind of those on both ends of spectrum? Do fans need a space where they can just be fans without any worry of creators seeing what they are doing? How do fans tackle issues of inappropriate behaviour within their own fandoms? And what happens when fans move out of the fandom sphere into being creators in their own right?

Crossing the Line

In 2022 a Netflix adaptation of the book *Heartstopper* by Alice Oseman became one of the most watched shows in the UK. It tells the story of a gay teenage boy and his crush who is coming to terms with his own sexuality as a bisexual. It's a teen romantic drama, that will warm you to your cockles but it hit the news feeds for all the wrong reasons.

After several months of constant messaging, comments, Twitter threads and even attacks on his safety, one of the actors, Kit Connor left social media. Why? Because he had been accused by fans of the show of playing a queer character while not being queer himself – something that should never have been an issue in the first place. The onslaught forced Connor to come out, despite he, himself saying that he wasn't ready to do so, in order to try and end the stream of abuse.

In the last few years, social media has helped the walls between fandom and creator spaces are become more and more blurred and giving fans this level of access to creators, and some fans take that too far. Think about how the stars of reality shows like *Love Island* are treated on social media, or many of the actors from *Star Wars,* or the way that Tumblr users bullied author John Green off the site. Connor is far from the only one to be placed in this sort of position by fans of the media that he was in but it shouldn't have happened to any of them.

The uncertainty of where the line of fandom sits means that sometimes fans go too far and it's hard to come back once that has happened. But it's not all one way.

It's a pretty common sight these days to see fans and creators all engaging with fandom on the same platform. Places like Twitter have made it so that the coffee houses and salons of the past are starting to be replicated online. Fans are able to directly ask their favourite creators, actors and musicians about the media they create in a similar, intimate way that fans of Byron and his ilk would have been able to around coffee and candle light. Except Twitter is much bigger than a room in a house in London in the 1800s and a lot more anonymous.

It can be encouraged, with creators setting up Discords, Reddit forums or Patreons for their fans to get closer access, in order to build a community and it is, for the most part, a positive thing for all involved. However, much like when fans get to close to creators, the same can happen in reverse and lead to some of the stranger moments in fandom history and years of debate about how much fans and the people they are fans of should interact.

Have you heard the story of the fandom that disappeared? It's a tale passed down the generations of fans, a loose thread of the great tapestry of fandom folklore, about a once-thriving fandom that vanished in the blink of an eye, leaving little but a few dead forums and a single message.

> '[This] page is no longer in the public forum. Note. There's nothing here. No specs, no stories, no nothing. Now maybe, hypothetically, if you had the password and the handshake you could get into the private forum where private citizens could still share private words with each other without being told by authors with too much money to waste that their amendment is being taken away and of speech no longer exists. But that's just hypothetical.'
>
> *The Main Page of the 'VC Spec Archive'*

In the year 2000 a whole fandom all but ceased to exist because, allegedly, the author of the original works decided that she didn't want people making fanfiction about them. This is the story of Anne Rice and so called 'Specs Writer Massacre'.

You might be forgiven for thinking that there isn't much of a fandom for the Anne Rice *Vampire Chronicles (VC)* books, the most famous being *An Interview With The Vampire,* or at least a few years back you would have. Considering the popularity of the books and films, which are genuinely worth picking up for a night of gothic romance and fun, it would have been a bit of a surprise to see that very little fanfic, or specs – short for speculative – as the fandom called them, and fanart existed of them at one point in time. This is due to the fact that many fan creators were, allegedly, contacted by the lawyers or associates of Anne Rice and told to remove their works from the internet or face legal action.

According to those affected writers, big name fans and forum admins received cease and desist letters from Rice's legal team. It is reported that in some cases this involved private information about small businesses belonging to fans. Since none of the fans had the ability to risk being taken to court, they all took down their works and choose to hide them away, deep in private servers, or just deleted them forever.

It would seem Fanfiction.net was also contacted and the entire archive of *Vampire Chronicles* and all other fanfics for Anne Rice properties were removed from the site without warning.

A message was posted to Anne Rice's official website that read:

'I do not allow fan fiction. The characters are copyrighted. It upsets me terribly to even think about fan fiction with my characters. I advise my readers to write your own original stories with your own characters. It is absolutely essential that you respect my wishes.'

This post was still on the website in 2023.

There is a reason why many fanfictions and other fanworks in the '00s and '10s had tags and notes on them with the phrase 'I do not own or claim to own any of the characters depicted in this piece of fan work' or something of the sort. Whatever had happened to the *VC* fandom sent shock waves through the whole fandom community, with many others fearing that authors or larger companies might do the same.

A creator had, supposedly, come into a fan space and demanded that the fans behave in a way that they, the creator, felt was appropriate. By doing so this broke the trust of not just the fandom in question but of fandom as a whole. Of course, it got out. People from the *VC* fandom weren't only fans of one thing, many went to other fandom boards or groups and told them what had happened. In other cases, people discovered that fanfic archives and blogs that they had been visiting for years as a more casual fan were just gone. The news spread through fandom to fandom until it became a thing of legend, the fandom that was lost. And it hurt. Fans no longer felt safe in their own forums and spaces.

To this day people still talk about this moment. It's a cautionary tale to fans to keep safe, to keep fandom spaces distanced from creators where needed or they might lose what they have, but times have changed and the relationship between fans and creator has changed with it. Whilst every so often a company or creator will purge works that breach copyright by being for sale on large-scale printing websites like RedBubble or Printful, it is rare to see a creator be anything more than overjoyed to see fanworks of any kind made of their work, but that doesn't mean that this should be forgotten.

Anne Rice passed away in 2021, and there has been a new TV show released since then that has brought in new fans and helped old ones come out of the woodwork. Beautiful art, fanfiction and other fanworks, have started to grow again in this barren corner of fandom but the urban legend of the 'Spec Writer Massacre' still hangs as a heavy weight over the fandom and will most likely remain that way for a long time to come.

Finding a point of co-existence is the ultimate achievement for a fandom. Sometimes that is never interacting with the creators at all, hiding away behind coded tags or in locked Discord channels, for others it's being a space curated by the creators themselves with moderators and admin making sure it all flows together, for some it's the creators never once stepping foot in the space the fans have no matter how public it is. However, for the fandom to work, it needs to enjoy and maintain respect from both sides or else that way madness, and Twitter dogpiles, lie.

Remember Wheaton's Law, from Wil Wheaton off that there *Star Trek: The Next Generation,* in all fandom spaces and no matter who you are: 'Don't be a d*ck'.

A Middle Way

'It's been a while,' I say to the Zoom call, 'how have you been?'

'Good! Nice to chat up!'

My call is with a long-time friend who, as is the way of these things when you are an adult, I had drifted apart from. Her name is Bria LaVorgna and she is one of the people who, probably without realising it, really got me into *Star Wars* in my late teens and early twenties. She's a journalist and blogger who now works for StarWars.com having written for a number of fan-blogs and other fan projects for some years, before moving from being a fan to being part of the big *Star Wars* machine proper. It is delightful to be able to use this book as an excuse for a catch up and chat fandom like old times before getting down to the brass tacks of what it's like moving across the streams.

> 'When you start writing officially you have to sort of, I don't want to say change, but sort of moderate your behaviour a little bit more,' Bria says. I can see peaks of *Star Wars* merch around her office along with a load of other fandoms making their way in the side of the camera box. 'I'm still obviously talking about the things I care about, being "I want to see more things" but I don't swear on Twitter anymore. Usually. Unless *Dragon Age* is like "by the way we're doing a TV series" and then I forget to moderate.'

It's a hard line to walk, being a fan of something while you are literally working for the company that produces it, and a harder one when you have something of a name for yourself before then. Keeping the persona of the known fan within a fandom that people enjoyed the views and works of whilst still toeing the company line is a tough one, even for someone like Bria who's been working as a journalist and been a known fan for some time.

For her, as with many fans who move from one side of the line to the other, it is still a shock to be seen as more than someone who enjoys their media of choice and is vocal about it, but who has now become a cog in the creation of that, or other, media, no matter how big or small that part is.

> 'I'm not a big-name fan I do a little bit of everything. And perhaps if I had focused on either cosplay, or I had just focused on writing, I would be more of a BNF. More like, a known commodity. I'm certainly known, I have people come up to me at Celebration and be like "Hi, like, big fan of your work" which is extremely funny when I'm standing with someone like Kristen Baver, who is you know, the face of *Star Wars* right now on YouTube? Or like Adam Christopher? Oh, just like, I was like, you have a book coming out next month, why are people talking to me? This is so weird.'

In part the balance of fan and creator is about loving the place you're in and still having that love for the people who are doing the making with you, whilst acknowledging that you, as strange as it may be, are doing the job too. For fans like Bria, and others, the way to find that middle ground and to keep up the balancing act isn't to be a fan making the work, it's being a fan of the work that you, yourself is making. People won't feel the love if you aren't putting it into the melting pot in the first place.

> 'I think the best way someone described it to me was someone who went from being a fan to working for [*Star Wars*], like employee badge working. He was just like, look at the people who are doing the things you want to do. See how they interact with other people. And look at the people who want to do what you want to do and don't. And I was like, that's a good point, he's right. I think what I realised is I'm not necessarily interested in being a being a *Star Wars* journalist who just talks about *Star Wars* all the time. Like, I don't really need to be the person analysing everything I'm much more interested in, not to go Alexander Hamilton, but I want to create something that's going to outlive me, I'd rather be a part of that team than talking about it.'

Look at any piece of media that has appeared in the last, well, forever, and you can see what and who the creators are fans of. They don't need to be working on a large-scale pre-existing piece of media like *Star Wars* for their own fandoms to shine through. Of course, we are all influenced by things, the overt and obvious references to fandom in shows, books, or pretty much any piece of media you could point at really show how much people love to be fans and want to be fans at the same time as being creators. This isn't the same as the wink-wink, nudge-nudge pop culture references of the likes of *The Big Bang Theory* or the *Shrek* franchise, it's a moment of 'you know what I'm showing you because you love it too and we can share in that love together'.

But being a fan and being involved in the creation of the media doesn't mean you always have to agree; it can be better if you don't. Having people who can understand the nuance of what the fandom is saying, whilst also understanding what is coming from the projects themselves can ease that middle path further. Having your own informed opinions as a fan and creator can lead to a very different point of view than if you sit on either side of the line.

For Bria she has managed to find a way to walk that line, giving her opportunities to work in the industry whilst being a fan at the same time. It's tricky, particularly when boundaries are being pushed from all sides over what a fan should and shouldn't have say in and how to be a fan at all.

'There's a delicate line between being like not eating your own, but also like not subscribing to a false sense of force; everyone must be positive about things all the time. There should be a line for critique, and there should be a way to do it respectfully. Like, I have issues with *The Mandalorian*, and *The Book of Boba Fett*, like I have issues with certain things on the shows, I do. I mostly keep them to myself, because I would like to continue to work [laughs]… I guess it's for me going from a fan to semi-professional with a has been doing good work. I'm showing I'm dependable. And then hopefully continuing to do more [for *Star Wars*].'

HUH?

No One Expects the Fandom Inquisition

In 2014 a monumental explosion happened within the gaming community, spreading across fandoms and eventually crashing out into the pop culture world as a whole, but it's likely that anyone outside of geekdom has never heard of it: this was GamerGate. It was the unexpected result of years of pressure being built up in the gaming community at large but forced into being by a much smaller subset of gamers with their own upsetting ends in mind.

It led to mass doxing, death threats, careers and lives being destroyed, and battle lines being drawn amongst fans. It was a major sign that fandom was different now, and that the way that fandom spaces had changed into open social media sites, rather than the closed forums and chat groups of the past, had pushed different groups into a melting pot like never before. But these were all fans, they all liked the same things and shared the same love for gaming, storytelling and the rest, so why would them coming together like this cause such an awful problem?

But fandom can be more than just enjoying something, or in many ways that enjoyment can lead to bigger, sometimes better, sometimes bitter, things. When you bring any group of people together there's going to be disagreements, what was it I said earlier about yelling about canon and storming out of a cave? Yeah, it's that, fans of any given thing are a single borg like blob that always agrees, always moves as one, always has all the same opinions, in fact it you'd think it was easy enough to see that there as many different ideas about a piece of media as there are different fans of it. No one agrees 100 per cent, but we'd be forgiven for thinking that fans could be organised as a mass of angry bots, yelling about how unhappy they are, when in reality that's just the loudest folks, splashing everyone as they flail around in the deep end.

Fans often sit at the head of what is being called 'The Culture Wars' and GamerGate is certainly a major moment in that, and while some fandom infighting can be more about your favourites holding hands or not, a lot of it ends up coming down to these much bigger, and more societal topics.

For many the need to see social change within their fandoms and the media they love is just as important as the things themselves, if not more so, and supporting that change to make pop culture more inclusive is an uphill fight they are happily willing to take on and have been for years across fandom spaces. But there are those who see this as unnecessary, even invasive, of their ideas and the spaces that they have long held to be their own, unable to see opening up the doors to different people as anything other than a loss of control. And thus, they clash.

That being said, fans can and do band together in all sorts of ways to do more, push what they expect out of the media they love, and to aim to improve popular culture as a whole. Since many fans are in this cultural vanguard, having been early adopters of digital spaces, or are now those young activists crying out for change, what they are doing and saying about where popular culture and media should be going is worth paying attention to. You can see the political and ideological divides show up time and time again, and how hard it is for people to challenge themselves on what they believe when it comes to their favourites, their blorbos. We're all guilty of it from time to time.

There is more to fandom than the sharing of fanworks and meta discussions, which can be interesting, certainly, and definitely lead to big changes in the world around them beyond that of their own fan space and even beyond the fan sphere entirely.

Culture Wars: GamerGate

Show of hands who's heard of GamerGate? Okay, that's, some of you. Show of hands who knows what actually happened? Less hands, okay, okay. And who knows about what came after? Right, a bit more in the dark. Good thing I brought a torch then to shine a light on this less-than-shining moment in fandom's recent history.

It all started in 2014, or at least the campaign that was later dubbed GamerGate began in August of that year. The culture of online harassment is as old as the internet itself, but with the online population growing and more and more differing groups of people becoming more prominent, in particular minority groups raising their voices to be heard and pushing to be taken seriously, this culture has become ever more intrenched and toxic. These are the culture wars.

The term 'Culture Wars' has been used in the media as a pretty catch-all phrase for pretty much every major moment of discourse over the last few years, ranging from the most serious of topics and politics all the way to over-blown mole hills that those looking for a click-bait headline have turned into mountains. It's hard to know what it means beyond making a good sound bite but at the heart of it, it's picking up on the very distinct clashes of groupings in online spaces often due to what we have already spoken about, the overwhelming nature of everyone being in a space together.

But back to GamerGate.

The name refers to an online harassment campaign predominantly against feminists, activists and minority groups working in gaming during the period of 2014–2015, spearheaded by groups on the forum websites, 4chan and Reddit, in order to stop the changing nature of videogames becoming more inclusive. There had been growing unrest in this area for some time, but it was in August 2014 that the flashpoint came that set the stage for GamerGate and what has followed. Time for a quick run-down montage of the major moment.

On the 14 August 2014 former boyfriend of the game developer and feminist Zoë Quinn posted a rant 'essay' about her onto a wordpress, called 'The Zoe

Post', after he had previously tried to post it to another website and been banned for doing so.

'The Zoe Post' made claims about Quinn cheating in order to gain better jobs, reviews and career prospects, all of which were debunked later by the same ex. The post about Quinn was shared by Quinn's ex-boyfriend to 4chan, a forum website known for a culture of anonymity, and a group began to rally around it in order to attack Quinn and their 'social justice warrior' friends. This was swiftly spread to Reddit and the harassment of Quinn began to grow with the goal of destroying their career alongside threats of doxing, that were carried out, with the group believing 'The Zoe Post's' claims.

'The Zoe Post' was a spark into the frustrations and anger that had been building, unchecked, for some time within certain sections of the gaming community and the chance was seized to take out those frustrations on someone who was seen to 'deserve' it in some way.

Of course others involved in the gaming community stood up for Quinn, notably Polytron founder Phil Fish and members of the *Kotaku* editorial and writing staff, but this ended up with them being harassed themselves and in Fish's case, doxed.

This all led to 4chan closing down the boards responsible, as well as lawyers becoming involved, and the group going deeper into the underground of the internet. Throughout all of this Quinn and their family were harassed, attacked and stalked, with doxing, threats of violence and constant online abuse being targeted at them. And it wasn't just Quinn who was under attack either.

Other prominent feminists in the gaming community were in the firing line as well, including journalist and video essayist Anita Sarkeesian, and game developer Briana Wu, who had written on news website Polygon about her experience as a woman in gaming and the abuse she had received because of it well before GamerGate had raised its head as a movement.

Sarkeesian was well known for her 'Women in Video Games' series on YouTube. Sarkeesian was, like Wu, already a target for online trolls and hate, being outspoken about the sexism that she observed in the video game industry both in and out of the games themselves. In August 2014 she was also made a target of those who had grouped together on 4chan, receiving death treats and having to leave her home in fear after contacting the FBI due to the high level of danger that the threats put her in. It was a dire, and disturbing, situation for both Sarkeesian and Quinn, who also later revealed that they had fled their home.

This all happened in less than a month. Somehow this had gone from what was a cruel post from an ex-boyfriend to a full-blown online hate campaign against feminism and representation in videogames, with Quinn, Sarkeesian, Wu, and anyone who stood up for them in the firing line, and all before the hashtag #GamerGate was even coined. That happened on 27 August, thirteen days after 'The Zoe Post' was made, and widely credited to actor Adam Baldwin who was tweeting in support of the campaign against Quinn, attaching #GamerGate to his tweet.

Over the next few days, the hashtag gained more and more traction. Those who rallied behind it claimed victories as their targets left social media, or even disappeared from the industry entirely, and it only got worse as fuel was added to the fire by far-right online commentators, like Milo Yiannopoulos who not only wrote continuously on the topic but also accused Quinn of embezzling funds from their company and Sarkeesian of making false claims in police reports. Both of these accusations are quickly found to be untrue.

Days of attacks became weeks, became months with the gaming community becoming increasingly more divided and the level of abuse rising with each new 'victory' that the GamerGate group felt they had over the 'SJW's. Restraining orders were issued by those at the heart of the abuse but many still feared for their safety and the future of the gaming industry as a whole. Even major entities like Wikipedia weren't immune to the ire of the GamerGate group, who flooded the site with edits and then, when the edits were removed, turned their gaze onto the founder and editors of Wikipedia.

By November pretty much every gaming company, website, and news outlet was reporting on #GamerGate and there was no part of the gaming world that didn't know what was happening. It was getting increasingly more widespread, with over a million tweets with the hashtag used in September alone and increasingly more tangled in a web of hate campaigns, anonymity and legal involvement with no end in sight.

The hate campaign continued for another two years, with Quinn, Sarkeesian and Wu remaining the main targets, with a number of serious attacks on their safety and their families over that period including an attempt by GamerGate to get Quinn and Sarkeesian arrested, but many, many others were targeted throughout these two years. The GamerGate group, still organising itself through sites like Reddit, 4chan and 8chan, turned on any and all developers, writers, companies or simply outspoken individuals who advocated for diversity in gaming with the same methods it had used against its initial victims.

But why did it all happen in the first place? Why was there a pyre this big ready to burn when 'The Zoe Post' was posted?

In the book *Cheating* by Mia Consalvo, she talks about the idea of social capital amongst gamers and how the gamer industry used this as part of their way of marketing. Essentially you can build yourself up in the community, your kudos and creditability as a gamer, obviously by showing how good you are, but the way that it was marketed was highly gendered. It was a boys' club, masculinised by both the companies and the players, and so the gamer guys became the target audience for most games, to the extreme in many cases, and many of them felt a sense of ownership over gaming as a culture. It became hyper masculine in a very toxic way with sexism and aggression playing key roles in the way that gamers spoke with each other while gaming or in forum spaces.

Consalvo theorises that when women gamers started to become a more obvious presence within gaming, because there have always been women in gaming – they just struggled to be noticed by the culture and the companies, the market had to change, and that shifted the social capital of the community as well and that may have meant that the boys' club felt a threat to the power that they had in this community. And thus, the frustrations began.

You can see how members of a community may have felt like they were losing their grip on the social capital and community space that they had and looked for someone to blame, a scapegoat. It ended up being women, feminists, and minority groups in the gaming community, as those who were seen as 'taking away' what they had.

But it wasn't just about gamers.

Many of those involved in GamerGate were members of forums and groups connected with conspiracy theories, the alt-right and hate groups. The growing unrest in the gaming community, and the culture that had grown around it, had meant that they were primed for these sorts of ideas and waiting for something to set off the trigger. The links between GamerGate and the alt-right were pointed out in the early days of the harassment campaign and the ties only got stronger as it continued.

In 2017 Zoe Quinn wrote a book on their experiences throughout GamerGate and how to deal with the type of online harassment that they faced. In it they stated:

'GamerGate wasn't really about video games at all so much as it was a flash point for radicalized online hatred that had a long list of targets before, and after, my name was added to it. The movement helped solidify the growing connections between online white supremacist movements, misogynist nerds, conspiracy theorists, and dispassionate hoaxers who derive a sense of power from disseminating disinformation. This patchwork of Thanksgiving-ruining racist uncles might look and sound like a bad joke, but they became a real force behind giving Donald Trump the keys to the White House.'

In 2021 connections from GamerGate were found to the storming of the Capitol in Washington DC, and 2022 the right wing conspiracy theorist David Depape, who attacked the husband of Speaker of the House Nancy Pelosi, Paul Pelosi, confessed to having being radicalised by GamerGate. One of GamerGate's major targets, Brianna Wu, who is now running for a Congressional seat, said to PBS News Hour:

'...everything I tried to get the FBI to act on in the aftermath of GamerGate has now come true... We told people that if social media companies like Facebook and Reddit did not tighten their policies about these communities of organized hate, that we were going to see violent insurrection in the United States... We told people that these communities were organizing online for violence and extremism. That, unfortunately, has proven to be true.'

It would be the easiest thing to write off GamerGate as rabid fans going rogue, calling it the fault of violent video games and gaming culture, but it wasn't. A culture of 'bro mentality' opened the door to hate, conspiracy theories and mass online abuse movements that has not been closed and in many ways has become legitimised within fandom. The 'Culture Wars' are well and truly part of fandom, in more ways than one.

Have A KitKat

So...

That was a lot. I don't blame you if you'd like a little break now; cup of tea and biccy, walk around a little maybe.

We'll regroup in five.

The Fall Out

Everyone back? Yes? Alright then, let's continue.

It would be nice to say that GamerGate is nought but dust in the distant internet past, but that would lying. Over the last few years there have been many similar pushes in this vein against inclusive changes in media.

You would have to be a hermit, living up a mountain, in the back of a cave to not have had the culture wars become part of your everyday life in some way. Round table discussions focused on cultural tensions on the news, movements against minority groups becoming mainstream, conspiracy theories filling up newsfeeds and inflammatory points of view being shared for the algorithms, it's overwhelming to the extreme and it's only been growing stronger within fandom spaces since GamerGate.

Online movements such as ComicsGate, Not My Doctor, the petitions against the casting of people of colour in films like *Star Wars* and others all spawned out of the space that GamerGate created, a space where all these things could happen and people felt were okay to do. It's encouraged by vocal supporters of the far-right who have spotted fandom spaces as a place to sow the seeds of political discourse much as they did with gamers. Social media and online spaces enabled those intent on causing harm or spreading conspiracy theories and alt-right ideas across the whole world in a way that was unheard of even a few decades ago, in a way that the companies running these online spaces may never have thought of, and it has caused definite harm to the fandom community. A major rift in fandom opened up and is still opening with the tremors felt throughout fandom communities. When I spoke with Professor Paul Booth of DePaul University, Chicago, he pointed out to me:

'[F]andom as much as it is a wonderful and unique experience for a lot of people is also subject to and part of the cultures that it emerges from. We live in a highly polarised, argumentative, antagonistic culture at the moment, so it makes sense that that's going to feed into fandom. It's not enough to just say, like, I disagree with you, let's talk about it, now. It's that you are problematic, you are cancelled, goodbye. And that happens in politics, and it's happening in culture, and it's happening in fandom, that a lot of that is perpetrated by social media. And it's not social media's fault, *per se*. It's the social media, kind of what I was saying before, it's controlled by corporations that are deliberately channelling and focusing the types of conversations that can be had. I mean, it has been conclusively proven that Facebook has manipulated people to make them more antagonistic on their site. I don't, I don't think Twitter has deliberately done that. But I think that the formatting of Twitter doesn't help. So is the affordances of social media reward people for more and more inflammatory kind of words.'

And Paul isn't the only fandom academic to be noticing this. It would be worrying if he was.

'It's almost like fandom has become a sort of cultural battleground for some of these things in GamerGate where that really became spectacularly kind of visible.'

Professor Matt Hills, and other academics, have looked into GamerGate and the fallout it caused over the last few years.

> Professor Hills commented: '[I]t almost then forms a template for people to organise, right wing reactionary kind of forms of resistance to commercial popular feminism, and commercial, popular social justice.
>
> There are other kinds of political actors, who are, who have a certain cultural politics who are explicitly anti-feminist in terms of their cultural position, and they seek to exploit and foment and instrumentally make use of tensions that are pre-existing in the fandom and kind of move into the fandom.'

When in 2017 Jodie Whittaker was announced to be the first woman to play The Doctor, voices not dissimilar to those involved in GamerGate appeared, creating a wave of discord through the *Doctor Who* fandom, buoyed up by the continuing ripples of anti-social and anti-progressive ideas.

'You had some people trying to gain a foothold in terms of, you know, being anti-feminist and anti-Jodie Whittaker, and anti-Chris Chibnall for his version of the show, and they try to coalesce around a sort of banner of of the NMD's or the Not My Doctors, you know, the death of *Doctor Who*, Jodie Whittaker isn't my doctor, and I'm anti all of this.' Matt says, a life long fan of *Doctor Who* himself as well as a fandom scholar. He says that *Doctor Who* fans have tended to be left leaning but even in a fandom like this, the fall out of alt-right players gaining a foothold in fandom spaces was felt across the board.

> Professor Hills continues: 'There's a sense in which we don't just maybe have a sort of the Tumblr version of multi fandom and fluidity, moving

across fandoms. If fandom itself can be fluid in that in that way, then there's also a fluidity to these other powerful discourses in contemporary culture. The culture war type label, where you've got people to also try and almost surf fandoms or move across and traverse different fandoms, trying to kind of develop certain flashpoints and tensions. And usually, in misogynistic ways, you know, really trying to kind of bolster anti-feminist and anti-social justice, and it can be based around race as well as gender.'

But it's not all doom and gloom, the push back in fandom spaces has come in just as readily as those trying to pull it apart, and a large part of that is fans using their buying power and putting their money where their mouth is. Campaigns to go out and watch female and POC-led superhero movies to make sure that they are seen in the box office figures are part of the ongoing movement to get fans to do more than tweet about the issues. Watching, sharing and putting social pressure behind TV shows like *Our Flag Means Death*, *The Owl House*, *Amphibia* and others with inclusive casts, storylines and creative teams, both because they enjoy them and because fans want to encourage more inclusive media. There's a lot to be said for being vocal online but often, it's the bottom line that makes a difference to what is produced so viewing figures, merchandise sales and box office revenue is often the best way for fans to make a point.

The same is true of gaming where hashtags like *Assassin's Creed* Sisterhood have trended with art, cosplay, fanfiction and more to bring about group efforts to change how women in gaming franchises are treated. Mass walk outs at companies against sexism, racism and anti-LGBTQIA+ feeling have forced change from inside the industry with fans supporting those taking a stand.

GamerGate was a turning point in fandom in the era of social media and the culture wars. It divided fandom like never before and drove groups that were already struggling to understand each other further apart. But that turning point as also meant that change, real substantial change, is starting to be seen through the actions of fans who were not about to lay down quietly under the attacks of those who intended to control and destroy the fandoms, creators and media that they loved.

Change My Dear and Not a Moment Too Soon

During my time on Tumblr I have seen many social justice issues discussed, argued about, and brought to bear as topics of import, but none so amusing or entertaining as what became known as 'The Hawkeye Initiative'. A move to point out how ridiculous the outfits worn by female superheroes were and call to arms by fans to change the representation of these characters, both in the comics and on screen through the medium of drawing Hawkeye – the one with the bow and arrow in *The Avengers* not the one from *M*A*S*H* – in the many absurd outfits and poses that female heroes were drawn in.

It took over comics Tumblr for a time. Every new cover or panel that came out with another thong-backed costume, sprayed-on suit or any generally sexist posing, 'The Hawkeye Initiative' was on it. The artists on Tumblr were having a field day, week, months, years with it. It was a laugh, but it was also a protest. Fans had had enough and they were going to make it known. People had been saying for years that they wanted change in the industry but it had fallen on deaf ears, but with the 'The Hawkeye Initiative' it became harder and harder to ignore as the thousands of images that were created for it went viral, with people even cosplaying as some of them. They still do. It became the buzzword for talking about the changes that were needed to drive out this form of sexism in the comics industry.

It did, as you can imagine, draw the attention of those involved in the likes of GamerGate, but that didn't stop the fans and creators pushing for the changes. Conventions ran panels on the subject, people made video essays, blogs were written, news sites reported on it. It couldn't be silenced or ignored – The Initiative was too far spread.

In 2012, Carol Danvers aka Ms Marvel, later to become Captain Marvel of Marvel Comics, was given a redesign. Her outfit was changed from a long, flowing blonde hair and black, skin tight swim suit style costume that left you wincing at the wedgy it gave, to a practical full body suit in the same vein as Captain America, a helmet and a haircut. It was designed by artist Jamie

McKelvie, and marked the first major change in the design for female superheroes in mainstream comics. Carol was followed by several major character redesigns including Wonder Woman and Power Girl at DC comics and the introduction of a new Ms Marvel alongside Carol: Kamala Khan, a young Pakistani girl whose costume was based around more traditional Pakistani clothing. The fans had been listened to and there was no turning back now.

What 'The Hawkeye Initiative' showed was the power that fans had and have to make progressive changes in their culture when they organise themselves, and particularly when they do so in a fannish way. It's something that can be visible, can be understood and can make a point of targeting companies, industries and politics in a way that no one else can.

The ARMY vs Trump

K-Pop. It's swept through the music industry and taken the world by storm. There are legions of fans of the genre, all over the planet, making the Korean idols who make up K-Pop superstars. The most famous of these bands, and the one that it would be hard not to have heard of even if you've been a hermit in a cave for the last few years, is BTS.

BTS are not a K-Pop group that has come out of the regimented and strict idol training in Korea, performing elaborate dance numbers as they sing and rap in a perfect harmony of teenage fantasy and musical brilliance. They are the dream boys following in the well-trod path of the likes of One Direction, Take That, Duran Duran and The Beatles. The music videos and live performances are works of art, bringing the songs to a new level of enjoyment for their fans, despite the fact that they are performed almost entirely in Korean and many of these fans are spread across Europe and the US. BTS are one of the first non-English speaking bands to chart in both the UK and the US, so yeah, they are a big deal. And their fans are something else.

K-Pop fans, specifically BTS fans, are known to have something of the Beatlemania fangirl about them. They love to buy and trade merch, always looking for items coming out of Korea to get their hands on, or the collaboration items with big name brands like Louis Vuitton, Puma and Hello Kitty, using BTS's own specialised merch designs as part of the campaigns. The fans love it and all the information about everything BTS is shared online, on TikTok, Twitter and on other fan pages. They know everything, all the time. It's definitely peak fandom behaviour and it's very, very organised.

These fans are like a military in their fannish ways so is it any surprise that they call themselves the ARMY.

It stands for 'Adorable Representative M.C. for Youth' though the other connotations are certainly present when you see how these fans organise themselves in and out of official fan spaces. Which brings me to Donald Trump.

A strange jump, certainly. What on Earth does ex-president and darling of QAnon, Donald Trump, have to do with K-Pop? Well, during the election cycle of 2020 Donald Trump was touring rallies around the US, with the venues and dates freely available for anyone to find to book their own tickets, something that the ARMY found quite interesting themselves.

Passing the word around through social media, mostly TikTok, and fan blogs, ARMY members began to book up the tickets for the Trump rallies in order to make it seem that they were sold out, but Trump would turn up to empty stadiums and his own supporters would be unable to attend. A small and simple act of political activism. The scheme spread fast and soon it wasn't just K-Pop fans doing it, thousands of young people were in on it, through the organised work of the ARMY. And it worked.

Trump turned up to rally after rally to find them nearly empty and the seats claimed by K-Pop fans all over the world, blocking him from speaking.

But this isn't the only time that K-Pop fans have organised themselves for the sake of activism.

The ARMY have been known to flood Twitter tags and force trending topics to get their favourites to the top of Twitter, but they have also used this technique to overload white-supremist tags in order to get them stopped, overwhelmed police hotlines searching for people involved in peaceful protesting, and spammed Donald Trump on multiple occasions, including on his birthday card in protest against his presidency.

K-Pop fans have found power in their fandom. The realisation that you can organise through fandom for mass political movement is one that can be used for good or ill, but the winds seem to be blowing in the direction of young fans like this, not only pushing fandom as activism but seeing that they can do more with the community that they have built.

Above: Anita Sarkeesian at the Game Developers Choice Awards, 2014. Image by Official GDC, Creative Commons BY 2.0.

Below: Ripple Effect: How Women-in-Games Initiatives Make a Difference, at the Game Developers Conference 2016, Stephanie Fisher, Zoë Quinn, Sagan Yee, Gemma Thomson, and Rebecca Cohen-Palacios. Image by Official GDC, Creative Commons BY 2.0.

Above: The audience at the Game Developers Conference Ripple Effect panel with Zoë Quinn. Image by Official GDC, Creative Commons BY 2.0.

Below: BTS at the White House. This band have definitely got a place on the global stage, just like their fans.

K-Pop World Festival in Korea. Image Korea.net Korean Culture and Information Service, Creative Commons BY-SA 2.0.

BTS ARMY fans at LGxBTS launch event, from the LG Electronics' official Flickr, Creative Commons BY 2.0.

3 Look Inside the House

Social progressiveness is very much a trademark of a current arm of fandom. Projects like 'The Hawkeye Initiative' didn't spring out of nowhere and gain traction without there being a bedrock of socially progressive thought already at the core of much of fandom. Take a look at *Star Trek* and *Star Wars* for example: both have, at the heart of their storytelling, progressive ideas and commentary on the world they were made in and that is reflected in most, if not all, of their fanbase. Comic books are the same, as is most science fiction, and even if some of the fandom misses the point, many learn the lessons and attempt to make positive changes in the world around them because of it.

However, this does not mean that fandom, all fandom, is without its faults.

For many people with progressive ideas, be they part of fandom or not, there can be a certain belief that you could never do anything wrong or make mistakes, which is simply not true. Humans do human stuff all the time, and it's okay to mess up, but it's how you react to it that can cause problems and this is something that is often an issue within fan culture when you put in the added layer of 'but this is my favourite thing' and all the emotions that go with it.

Fandom is a very emotional place, we've talked about that, how connected we as fans are with the stories and characters we love. It's hard to see criticism of those things or the way that we interact with them, which can lead to some kneejerk reactions or misunderstandings, but we do owe it to ourselves, our fellow fans, and the stories we love and admire to look inside the house and make changes.

In some ways this is obvious. Asking for sexist costumes to be redesigned, or for more characters of colour to be included in media, these are big and necessary changes that push back against conservative ideas and encourage inclusivity, but there are less visible things that need to be challenged too.

Dr Rukmimi Pande of O.P. Jindal Global University, New Delhi, is an academic studying minority groups within fandom and has written a book, *Squee from the Margins*, about the issues faced by marginalised communities with fan spaces. I spoke to her about the subject in mid-2022.

'I talked about this a little bit in the book that fandom sees racism as individual action, sees it as somebody who is a bad actor, who is breaking fandom rules, and is causing harm. And so sometimes those bad actors can be excluded. But when people start talking about patterns, for instance, then it starts becoming much more difficult because then people start saying, "oh, you just don't like the ship" but the ship is only an example. It's not as if people are talking about it, looking at one ship as the thing, they're talking about a broader product, a broader problem of how these things occurred.'

Racism, homophobia, sexism, all have patterns of behaviour outside of the obvious 'bigotry' we might associate with the likes of GamerGate and its ilk. But we are all guilty of them no matter how much work we do on ourselves. Humans can always learn and grow in their ideas, this is as true of fan spaces as it is of anywhere else. There are stereotypes that those of us within fandom spaces may not even recognise as being micro-aggressions or straight up bigoted behaviour because fandom is progressive in many ways, and because it's hard to see issues with the things you love and who shaped you as a person. Rukmimi tells me:

'As a young queer person growing up in India with not much access to you know, my family was generally a liberal family, but this wasn't something that ever was talked about, or there was, there wasn't any information. And I mean, for most of my life, it was it was illegal. So, you know, this, it was talking, figuring out queerness, figuring out, figuring out aspects of myself, is deeply bound up in fandom and I am a Kirk/Spock shipper, it was my original ship.

But I remember that when the when the *Star Trek* movie came out in 2009, and there were people were talking about the [racist] treatment of Uhura, by Kirk/Spock shippers, and I didn't want to think about that. I was, like, "no, no, this is not happening,", or "this doesn't say anything about me" but, thankfully, I suppose at that stage I listened and, and saw the validity of those critiques.

I say this because people seem to think that it's only about losing something. That if you engage with this process, you will be losing some kind of vanished joy, or it will be things that you cannot enjoy, you cannot take pride in anymore, or you cannot engage with, that everything will be bad. But I would say that moment that I had, that I understood what was happening, and I understood what people were saying, helped me engage with fandom spaces and characters in a more in a more grounded way.

I think there is a larger desire to one want one's fandom to reflect one's politics,' Rukmimi continues, 'and that's fine, it comes from a space of [positivity] but I think that becomes difficult, when you can't have it both ways. You can't have your fandom be reflective of yourself and also never want to question that.'

The fact that fandom does become part of us means that the moment it's questioned we are forced to question ourselves. It can be hurtful to have to reframe things that mean so much to you but as Dr Pande says, doing so can bring you a new view point on your fandom and yourself.

Fans being defensive of their fandoms is hardly new. 'Ship wars' or discourse about interpretation feel as though they have been part and parcel of fandom since the dawn of time, no matter what you think of them, but it also feels as if there is more at stake now with criticism of media being so public rather than in the private fan spaces of the past. Rukmini says:

'[It] has become so you can't critique a show, for instance, without some people saying that you are obviously trying to hurt that show in some way. And I think that's been tied to, you know, if somebody is mean about the show online, then that hurts the show's reputation, which is kind of, I think, a reflection of people being more aware than then earlier, about how these [fan] spaces are kind of monitored, monitored by companies.'

Companies and creators have been known to change things within a piece of media because of what they have seen in fandom spaces, including changing storylines due to people figuring out the 'twist', taking out characters or even straight up cancelling the show, and there are fans who want to use fandom as a shield of protection rather than as a place of discussion, learning and growing as people. Instead, this puts fans in a place of defensiveness, as it started with GamerGate, that can take turns into the nastier side of fandom without many of those involved even realising.

'I think what we do have is people tapping into fears that fandom has and are using it to fuel certain kinds of reactionary reaction to shut down any possible conversation that you could have about these issues, because you're already making it a such a polarised [thing] in such a weaponized space, that it's impossible to say something without it being misconstrued.'

This is something that I heard from almost everyone I spoke to while writing this book, and that speaks volumes of what fandom needs to do in order to come out of the culture wars and the current, political polarisation with that change for the better still blooming as part of what the community is.

We need to take time to listen to each other, take a breath and really listen beyond our kneejerk reactions to seeing our favourites critiqued. It's easier said than done, we all know that, it's hard not to want to defend something that is part of who you are as a person. Fandom runs deep, we know that. We all have room to grow and learn, and as Rukmimi said, it does not take away joy from you to see what you love in a different light and to see more clearly the view point of others. There is more to fandom than art and fics and video essays, more to it than canon and collecting. Fandom cannot be separate from the rest of the world, and nor should it be.

4 Learn From History or be Doomed to Repeat It

Fandom is an ever changing, growing and adapting space, and there is always space for all of us who live within it to not only grow with it but to shape the way that it does so. If everything that this part has talked about has said anything it's that we, as fans, are part of making sure that we see our media change and progresses in a way that includes everyone, no matter who they are. This does not mean that we should always be looking forward and not carrying the history of fandom and fan culture with us.

Knowing where your community came from and the ways in which people were part of the formative change that brought us to where we are today is important. You can't go forward if you don't learn from where you've come from.

It sounds intense but there are lot of people who come into fandom who have never learned the history that we went through at the front of the book, though I don't think you should have to pass an exam to be allowed in fandom. It's pretty useful to know that fandom existed before Tumblr, or LiveJournal or the internet, or TV, or anything that we would think of as fan culture now, because it grounds you. Being able to look back and see people like you, doing what you do gives you more of a sense of belonging than anything and it also helps you see the cycles that fandom goes through and hopefully helps stop mistakes repeating. Hopefully.

If we want to move forward in a positive way then looking for patterns in the history of a community is an important tool on our belt.

Fanlore

Go back to the beginning, read it all again and meet me back here. No, I'm joking, I mean, all that we went through was really just the dates and places in all honesty. We barely even scratched the surface of the deep and winding history that each and every fandom has in its own way. There is so much that happens from fan space to fan space, from group to group, that really the idea that all of it could be written down is almost unimaginable. Good thing we have places like Fanlore trying their best to keep it all going.

Fanlore is a public site, that anyone can make an account on, that documents fandom. It presents the people, the conversations, the essays, the vlogs, the 'zines, each fandom's discourse and prominent works as best it can. It's huge and a rabbit hole that, shockingly, I fell into a few times while writing this book. It is run by The Organisation for Transformative Works (OTW), alongside Ao3, and is for fans, by fans, archiving and updating their own history and communities. It's a hell of a project to undertake, let alone with volunteers all over the world.

This is the place to look for almost any fandom-related piece of history, almost. With the whole thing being voluntary, and fandom being, until very recently, an underground movement hidden in the secret corners of pop culture, there are gaps. Big ones that may never be filled as 'zines, newsletters and other physical fanworks disappear as those who made or kept them stop being involved in fandom for whatever reason, often, at this point in time, because they have passed away. It's why places like Fanlore are so important to making sure that the cultural history of fandom isn't lost, since so much of it is likely lost already through lack of curation and it being an oral history passed in stories and fables from fan to fan.

The *Fan Culture Preservation Project* is a venture set up in 2009 to preserve and archive fanworks from before the internet in an effort not to lose a large and important part of social history. It is run by the Organisation for Transformative Works, jointly with the University of Iowa's Special Collections Department and aims to collect as many non-digital items of fan culture as possible, including, but not limited to, con-badges, flyers, zines, merchandise and pre-digital newsletters, videos and fanfictions. This is one of the many fannish projects around the world attempting to stop fan history from disappearing in to storage boxes, thrown into tips or simply vanishing into thin air. The collection is still open to anyone who wishes to donate.

Alongside this there is also the *Media Fandom Oral History Project*. An undertaking of two fans, and OTW contributors, Morgan Dawn and Franzeska Dickson, with the support and backing of OTW itself, the *Media Fandom Oral History Project* aims to collect the testimonials of fans as recorded interviews in order to keep the stories of fans and fandom alive in their own words rather than text on a screen. It's a way to maintain the human connection that there has always been in fan community and keep us linked to the voices of those who built up the fan culture we and future generations of fans enjoy.

From the *Media Fandom Oral History Project*'s FAQ on Fanlore:

> 'Why Are We Recording Our Oral History: For many reasons, the first being that we think the media fandom community is full of creative, dynamic and noteworthy people who, for 40 years, have been doing something quite revolutionary: rather than passively sitting and staring at the TV or the movies, we've transformed what we've seen into millions of stories and hundreds of thousands of communities (both online and in person). Second, because what little fandom history is being preserved is often being preserved by non-fans, who peek through the cracks and often come away with a distorted picture of who we are. By recording our history using our own voices, we permanently shape our history. And last, because too often history focuses on bland events and dates. By asking fans at all levels to share their fannish memories, we can capture a broader range of who we are and what kind of communities we have created.'

Fanlore, however, does more than archive the physical examples of fanworks, it also holds archives on fan discourse across the decades, linking to or preserving essays, discussion threads, major fallouts in fandoms or with creators, alongside documentation of big-name fans or fan groups of the past who may no longer be remembered by those currently in a fandom. It is a reliquary of fandom past, teaching those who come to see it of what has changed, what has not and what may still need to have change wrought upon it.

Basically, it keeps a record of as much fandom drama as possible because without it how could we possibly know that people in the past were just as argumentative, ridiculous and in love with media as we are? When I say you could get lost on this site for weeks, I mean it. And you would learn so much more than you ever thought you could, or ever thought you needed to.

Moving away from the internet, there are archives at libraries and universities all over the UK, the USA and Europe, in fact all over the world, that hold onto fanworks, particularly 'zines. 'Zine libraries are springing up all over the place, collecting as many homemade, hand drawn and hand written works as possible in order to save the communal histories of fans, activists and artists from the last century, and give future historians a clearer and more in-depth view of what people were thinking and feeling in the twentieth and twenty-first centuries.

We are in the most literate point in human history, with almost universal access to tools to create, generate, and share our own ideas but if it's not saved outside of digital spaces than it may well be lost to time. The collecting and creation of physical items is more important than most people think.

The Lost Library of Cartoon Network

In the summer of 2022 a story broke that 36 animated shows were cut from Cartoon Network on HBO Max as part of a bid by the parent company, Warner Bros, to save money. They disappeared from streaming services overnight, some without having even being allowed to finish the seasons that were airing even if the animation itself was complete, others had multiple complete seasons removed without warning.

Not the end of the world you might think, you could just watch the shows elsewhere, but no. Many of the shows cut were exclusive to the HBO Max streaming service, which included not having any physical sales of DVDs or BluRay of the shows. This was the only place that they existed and then, they were gone.

The only thing that saved many of these shows from literally disappearing off the face of the planet was fans. Oh, and piracy. Digital piracy to be exact.

Since these shows were behind the pay wall of a streaming service, small bands of digital pirates, many of whom were fans of the shows, had spread copies around the internet onto archive video sites that host pirated TV and films. And yes, that is illegal, but, and it is a big but, what this illegal action did was stop 36 pieces of media from vanishing. They saved the hard work and hard-won projects of animators, writers and actors from being turned to ash.

Okay, but it's 'just cartoons', it's not important pieces of art or literature, but it could have been. With so much of our modern world only existing in online spaces, if and when those spaces cease to exist, or cease to be accessible due to the speed of technological advancement, it is very likely that we will loose a large amount of our own history, no matter how important those things are deemed to be. What happened at Cartoon Network was a glimpse at what could happen if companies decide that certain things aren't worth keeping and just push a button to get rid of it.

In this same clear out of Cartoon Network, it was discovered that the completed *Batgirl* movie, also made by Warner Bros, was cancelled and would not be released in theatres, with rumours being the film itself had been deleted. This was alongside archived episodes of the children's educational program *Sesame Street* being deleted from the HBO Max servers in order to cut costs despite the conscious effort to archive the show indefinitely.

Academics and commentators have theorised that we are going to enter a digital dark age due to the way that we are currently sharing and storing all our media as digital. We might be taking more photographs than any generation before us, or documenting more of our lives than has ever been possible, but that's not going to last if the moment YouTube's servers get shut down it's all lost. And it could happen so easily.

The work of fan pirates and fandoms to save media they love in this way, may well prevent that and has been proved to have done so many occasions even before the digital world existed.

The rediscovery of many lost episodes of *Doctor Who*, *Star Trek* and a myriad of other shows from when TV companies would reuse tape in order to save money happened because of fans would record the show off the TV in order to pass the episodes around to other fans in comic book shop lending libraries. Films that are no longer able to be accessed on streaming services and/or have been discontinued on physical media because they are no longer profitable are saved in the DVD and VHS libraries of avid film collectors and reuploaded to the internet or to physical archives in order to not be lost. Pirated recordings of radio shows and concerts that were never saved have been found in boxes in attics, storage containers and filing cabinets and added back into archives for posterity. And this all because fans went out of their way to save them even when no one else saw the value in doing so.

We take for granted the media that is given to us. We assume that we can log into a streaming service somewhere and find what we want to watch, listen to, or read, but that isn't always the case and may well become less and less the case in the coming years. Even archiving media digitally may not be enough to save it if it is only in one place in one way. Saving media across mediums and archives where possible is the best way to make sure that this doesn't happen and if that is done illegally, well, I can't comment but... it seems as if fans are doing it and that might just make some future historian's day.

THE END?

'We are each of us alone, what can you do but hold your hand out into the darkness...'

Ursula K. Le Guin, The Unreal and the Real: Selected Stories, vol. ii

Is that not what we're doing when we engage with fan spaces? When we open ourselves up to stories and all that come with them? Searching for meaning beyond ourselves? Making it in places where it was not there before? We are reaching out to others to make a point of contact, going out on our own deep space mission.

So why do we do it? Same reason anyone does anything: connection. Things change, you change, you grow up, what you loved to do as a kid might not be the same thing you loved to do as a teen and then you might swing right back round to those more childlike loves again as an adult. And you learn along the way what is important to you as a person because of the connections you made with others along the way, good, bad or ugly.

We find meaning in these things, add them to ourselves, beg, borrow and steal from them until they make up who we are as people. You can't know what parts of all the fandoms and communities you have been part of will serve you in making you who you are until you're there.

I had never intended on having so much of my own experience in this book, but, and I hope that you agree with me on this, reader, I found that it was impossible for that not to be the case. Fandom is connection and so why should it have been a surprise to find that, that connection appeared at each corner turned or stone uncovered. It's all very, well, human, I suppose, finding funny, little things to love and that help us bond with other humans. For all its faults and problems, fandom is very good at bringing us together and keeping us there.

When my dad read me *The Hobbit* there was no way I could know that it would be the thing that linked us so tightly to each other that on the day he died I would be sat, reading it to myself to find comfort in it. It became part of me that was him. That is what these stories do, they bind us to each other. We look at them like they are things for children, that it is somehow silly to still want to believe in fantasy as an adult, but it's okay that they are like that because without them, we lose our meaning. We are lost in the dark.

But my dear adventurers in fandom, it appears we have reached the end. Or an end of sorts at any rate, a place of parting ways. Hopefully you don't regret not picking up that Neil Gaiman book and instead continuing on this exploration, though there's probably a copy still in the shop if you fancy stretching your legs.

FURTHER READING

Question One

Jenner, Greg. *Dead Famous: An Unexpected History of Celebrity from Bronze Age to Silver Screen*. Orion Publishing Group, Limited, 2022.

Allan, Janice M., and Christopher Pittard, eds. *The Cambridge Companion to Sherlock Holmes*. Cambridge Companions to Literature. Cambridge: Cambridge University Press, 2019. doi:10.1017/9781316659274.

McDayter, Ghislaine. *Byromania and the Birth of Celebrity Culture*. Albany: State University of New York Press, 2010.

Brontë Babe Blog. *Brontë Babe Blog*, 2023. https://brontebabeblog.wordpress.com/

Glosson, Sarah. *Performing Jane: A Cultural History of Jane Austen Fandom*. Baton Rouge: Louisiana State University Press, 2020.

Lambert, James T., and Troy Lambert. *The Tao of Trek*. Indiana: Mooney and Lambert, 2022.

Duffett, Mark. *Understanding Fandom: An Introduction to the Study of Media Fan Culture*. New York: Bloomsbury Academic, 2013.

Booth, Paul. *Playing Fans: Negotiating Fandom and Media in the Digital Age*. Iowa City: University of Iowa Press, 2015.

Booth, Paul. *A Companion to Media Fandom and Fan Studies*. Chichester: Wiley Blackwell, 2023.

Question Two

Vivian Asimos. 2023. https://www.vivianasimos.com/.

Kies, Bridget, and Megan Connor. *Fandom, the next Generation*. S.l.: UNIV OF IOWA PRESS, 2022.

Hills, Matt. *Fan Cultures*. London: Routledge, 2005.

Jenkins, Henry. *Fans, Bloggers, and Gamers: Exploring Participatory Culture*. New York: New York University Press, 2006.

A Star Wars Fan Network. 'The Rexin around Show.' The Rexin Around Show. 2023. https://www.rexinaround.com/.

Questions Three and Four

Gray, Jonathan, Cornel Sandvoss, and C. Lee Harrington. *Fandom Identities and Communities in a Mediated World*. New York, N.Y: New York University Press, 2017.

DiPiazza, Francesca Davis. *Fandom: FIC Writers, Vidders, Gamers, Artists, and Cosplayers*. Twenty-First Century Books, 2018.

Busse, Kristina, and Karen Hellekson. *Fan Fiction and Fan Communities in the Age of the Internet: New Essays*. Jefferson: McFarland & Company, Inc., Publishers, 2006.

Jenkins, Henry. *Textual Poachers: Television Fans and Participatory Culture*. New York: Routledge, 2013.

The Stupendium. 'The Stupendium.' YouTube. 2023. https://www.youtube.com/TheStupendium.

Question Five

Waysdorf, Abby S. *Fan Sites: Film Tourism and Contemporary Fandom*. Iowa City: University of Iowa Press, 2021.

Stanfill, Mel. *Exploiting Fandom: How the Media Industry Seeks to Manipulate Fans*. University of Iowa Press, 2018.

Linden, Henrik, and Sara Linden. *Fans and Fan Cultures: Tourism, Consumerism and Social Media*. PALGRAVE MACMILLAN, 2018.

The Tosche Station. Toschestation.net. Accessed March 23, 2023. https://toschestation.net/.

Question Six

Quinn, Zoë. *Crash Override: How Gamergate Nearly Destroyed My Life, and How We Can Win the Fight against Online Hate*. Perseus Books Group, 2017.

Scott, Suzanne. *Fake Geek Girls: Fandom, Gender, and the Convergence Culture Industry*. New York University Press, 2019.

Pande, Rukmini. *Squee from the Margins Fandom and Race*. Chicago: University of Iowa Press, 2018.

Pande, Rukmini. *Fandom, Now in Color: A Collection of Voices*. Iowa City: University of Iowa Press, 2020.

Barnes, Renee. *Fandom and Polarization in Online Political Discussion: From Pop Culture to Politics*. Cham, Switzerland: Palgrave Macmillan, 2022.

Cook, Tanya, and Kaela Joseph. *Fandom Acts of Kindness: A Heroic Guide to Activism, Advocacy, and Doing Chaotic Good*. Dallas, TX: Smart Pop Books, an imprint of BenBella Books, Inc., 2023.

Booth, Paul J. 'Framing Alterity: Reclaiming Fandom's Marginality.' *Transformative Works and Cultures* 28 (2018). https://doi.org/10.3983/twc.2018.1420.

Booth, Paul J. 'Fandom: The Classroom of the Future.' *Transformative Works and Cultures* 19 (2015). https://doi.org/10.3983/twc.2015.0650.

GLOSSARY OF TERMS

Anime – Japanese animation medium spanning all genres.

Ao3 – Archive Of Our Own, an online fanfiction archive.

Blorbo – a favourite character.

BNF – acronym for Big Name Fan.

Comic Con – an umbrella term for all conventions and events.

Console – a computerised device designed for playing video games, can be static or hand-held.

Cosplay – short for costume play, a form of performance and craft-based fanwork revolving around dressing up.

D20 – a 20-sided dice.

Doxing – to search for and publish private or identifying information about a particular individual on the internet, typically with malicious intent.

E-Sports – Electronic Sports, competitive video gaming that is massively popular.

Fan – a person with a strong interest in or passion for something.

Fan Sphere – the metaphorical space that fans inhabit.

Fanart – art made by fans focused on the subject/s of their interests.

Fanboy – a fan who is a boy.

Fancasting – fans casting actors that they would like to see in film/TV/media adaptions of their favourite fandoms.

Fandom – the collective state of being a fan of someone or something.

Fanfiction – fiction written by fans.

Fangirl – a fan who is a girl.

Fanon – fan ideas or works that are considered canon by a majority of the fandom.

Fanwork – any works or creations by fans of their fandom.

Fanzine/'zine – collection of fanworks, printed as magazines.

Fav – short for favourite.

Femme-slash – slash fiction of female characters – *see* Slash.

FF.net – short for FanFiction.Net, an online fanfiction archive.

Filing Off The Serial Numbers – removing the obvious or copyrighted names, places, and other parts of a fanfiction in order to make it into original fiction.

Fourth Wall – the space that separates the performer, story and characters from the audience.

Gamer – a person who plays video games, can also refer to a sub-set of fans who self-identify as gamers.

Genderbending/changing – a fan changing a character who is in canon one gender to another.

Headcanon – ideas and concepts about a piece of media made by individual fans, it does not need to be supported by the original text or media.

Kaiju – giant beasts that come from the deepest depths of the Earth, often found in Japanese folklore, stories, movies and manga. Godzilla is a kaiju.

Manga – Japanese comics of all genres.

Merch – short for merchandise.

Multiverse – multiple universes of a single story or character that all run alongside each other, they may crossover in canon or in fanworks.

Nerdcore – a genre of music focused on 'nerdy' and fandom content, often using rap and hiphop as a style.

NOTP – No-OTP, a ship/pairing that you deeply dislike.

OTP – acronym for One True Pair, a fan's favourite ship/pairing.

OTW – Organisation of Transformative Works.

Queerbaiting – insinuating a character or relationship is queer/LGBTQIA+ but never confirming it in canon.

Racebending/changing – a fan changing a character who is in canon one race to another.

Ship/Shipping – a relationship between two characters that can be canon or not.

Slash – fanfiction focused around male homosexual couples, can be used as generic term with any queer ship. Also *see* femme-slash.

Squee – a 'sound effect' term used by fans to show excitement.

TTRPG – Tabletop Roleplaying Game.

Usenet – early internet platform.

Wattpad – a non-archival website used for writing and sharing fanfiction.